TABLE OF CONTENTS

ACRONYMS

AL	Alternative Livelihood
ASNF	Afghan Special Narcotics Force
CD	Counterdrug
CIA	Central Intelligence Agency
CN	Counternarcotics
CND	Counternarcotics Directorate
COIN	Counterinsurgency
CPEF	Central Poppy Eradication Force
CRS	Congressional Research Service
DEA	Drug Enforcement Agency
DOD	Department of Defense
DOJ	Department of Justice
DOS	Department of State
DS	Direct Support
FARC	Revolutionary Armed Forces of Colombia
FID	Foreign Internal Defense
FM	Field Manual
GWOT	Global War on Terrorism
HN	Host Nation
IA	Interagency
INL	DOS Bureau for International Narcotics and Law Enforcement Affairs
ISAF	International Security Assistance Force
JP	Joint Publication

NDCS	National Drug Control Strategy
NGCDSP	National Guard Counterdrug Support Program
NIU	National Interdiction Unit
OGA	Other Government Agency
SAS	Special Air Squadron
SF	Special Forces
SOF	Special Operations Forces
UK	United Kingdom
UNODC	United Nations Office on Drugs and Crime
US	United States
USAID	US Agency for International Development
VPTF	Vertical Prosecution Task Force

ILLUSTRATIONS

CHAPTER 1

INTRODUCTION

Successfully fighting the Global War on Terrorism (GWOT) requires the United

States "to disrupt and destroy terrorist organizations of global reach and attack their

leadership; command and control, and communications; material support; and finances"

(The National Security Strategy of the United States of America 2002, 5). One source of

funding for terrorist organizations is from the production and trafficking of illicit drugs.

Expounding on this concept, the Drug Enforcement Agency (DEA) states, "Whether it is

a state, such as formerly Taliban-controlled Afghanistan, or a narcoterrorist organization,

such as the FARC [Revolutionary Armed Forces of Colombia], the nexus between drugs

and terrorism is evident" (DEA Drug Intelligence Brief 2002).

Prior to 11 September 2001, the most visible aspect of this connection was

between the FARC and coca trafficking. US assistance to the Colombian government to

fight narcoterrorism at the time amounted to foreign aid, equipment, and a small

contingent of US advisors, mostly US special forces (SF) soldiers. Since 11 September

2001, the US government has focused on one of the major sources of funding for al

Qaeda: Afghan opium. Today, there are over 20,000 soldiers serving in Afghanistan,

training the Afghan National Army and conducting operations along the Afghanistan-

Pakistan border region. In 2004, Afghanistan provided 87 percent of the global opium

product. "The head of Afghanistan's Counter Narcotics Directorate [CND] estimates that

the Taliban and its allies derived more than $150 million from drugs in 2003" (Chouvy

2004, 3). Despite being vanquished from power in late 2001, the Taliban still operate in parts of Afghanistan and they still have strong connections with al Qaeda. However, relatively little is being done militarily to combat this aspect of the GWOT.

The former head of the DEA summarized the connection between terrorism and drug trafficking in remarks to the Congress, "[The] DEA has identified several of these terrorist groups that are associated with or directly engaged in drug trafficking. The events of September 11, 2001 graphically illustrate the need to starve the infrastructure of every global terrorist organization and deprive them of the drug proceeds that might otherwise be used to fund acts of terror" (Hutchinson 2002). While this statement from the DEA administrator focuses on how his organization can support the GWOT, the US military could be looking at how it can also support this aspect of combating terrorism.

In the contemporary operating environment the military opines about full-spectrum operations. Army Field Manual (FM) 3-07, *Stability Operations and Support Operations*, specifically addresses support to counternarcotics (CN) operations, as a mission of the Army. The Afghan government has enjoyed its first fully democratic elections in history. The Afghan National Army is trained and equipped and conducts operations in every province in the country. Yet Afghan opium harvests have increased as a percentage of world opium production from 79 percent in 1999 to 87 percent in 2004 (unless otherwise stated all data regarding poppy cultivation in Afghanistan come from the United Nations Office on Drugs and Crime (UNODC), *Summary Findings of Opium Trends in Afghanistan, 2005*). It should be noted that total world opium production did decrease 18 percent during this period, and total Afghan production decreased 8 percent, yet the problem remains that Afghanistan's opium production has increased as a percentage of global opium production. One might argue that the majority of coalition forces in this region are operating on the Afghanistan-Pakistan border, a mountainous region not conducive to poppy cultivation. However, the sheer quantity of acreage producing poppies is staggering: 131,000 hectares in 2004. Surely, the US-led coalition can assist the Afghan government in doing more without a detriment to the coalition's current operations.

Thus, the primary question to be answered is, Is the current model of interagency (IA) CN cooperation sufficient to have an impact on Afghanistan's opium dependency and disrupt one of al Qaeda's main sources of funding? One aspect of this thesis is to analyze the connection between narcotrafficking in Afghanistan and al Qaeda, and to determine what additional actions should be taken in this regard to combat terrorists. The secondary question addressed here is, Since CN operations are subordinate missions of special operations forces (SOF), how can SOF be used without detracting from their current activities? The tertiary question is, Is there a more efficient and effective method of employing IA or joint IA task forces in the CN role?

These issues are an important aspect to the GWOT, as highlighted in the National Security Strategy. Fighting the GWOT will take decades and it is essential to target all aspects of it. This thesis will focus on the application of military force in support of CN operations, although many dimensions of these operations fall into the IA arena. Therefore, only the IA aspects that directly fall into the tactical realm of CN operations will be addressed here. This includes the intelligence support from the Federal Bureau of Investigation, Central Intelligence Agency (CIA), and other government agencies (OGA) needed for ground forces to act upon. Additionally, the activities of the UNODC, creating and sustaining the Afghan institutions needed for ongoing CN operations, have a direct impact on ensuring that once US forces leave Afghanistan al Qaeda will not begin narcotrafficking once again.

Critics see many reasons to avoid adding CN operations to the military mission in Afghanistan. Two primary reasons deserve attention. First, because Afghan opium is the source of 90 percent of the heroin found on European streets, some feel that by failing to fully commit to a CN solution it is possible to extort the Europeans into a larger role in the stability and reconstruction operations in Afghanistan. Second, US CN operations have a dubious history. Most notable is the multidecade effort to assist the Colombian government in its crusade against coca production. In 1986, President Reagan declared war on narcotraffickers, and in 1988 President Bush released his Andean Strategy, a three-step program to decrease drug trafficking in the US. One aspect was to increase CN funding to fifty-sixty million dollars annually to Andean countries, primarily Colombia, Bolivia, and Peru. Another aspect was to conduct US operations unilaterally in Bolivia, then the highest producer of coca crops. Operation Blast Furnace was tactically successful; it shut down Bolivia's coca production for three months. The US destroyed crops and processing plants, captured producers, and succeeded in driving the supply side prices down from one-hundred twenty-five dollars to fifteen dollars, creating a net loss for producers. However, politically such actions could not be sustained, and after protests from Latin American countries such operations were cancelled. Two decades later, Latin America is still the number one coca producer despite years of foreign aid and US military and IA assistance. More importantly to this study, the FARC, once a purely Marxist political movement, is now a paramilitary organization that is primarily funded by narcotrafficking.

4

Similarly, the Taliban initially stated openly that opium production was intolerable. Mullah Omar, the Taliban leader, summarized the Taliban's position succinctly in 1977: "One thing, at least, is clear: we will permit neither opium nor heroin to be sold in Afghanistan itself. It is not up to us to protect non-Muslims who wish to buy drugs and get intoxicated. . . . Our goal for ourselves is to gradually eliminate all drug production in the country so as to safeguard our youth" (Torabi 1996-1997, 135-143). Slowly over the years, Omar began to see the possibility of funding his "freedom-fighters" against the invading Soviet Army through the proceeds of opium production. After the Soviets were defeated and the CIA stopped funding the mujahidin, Taliban leader Gulbuddin Hekmatyar continued to coordinate with the Pakistani intelligence service, "whose National Logistics Cell trucks delivered weapons to Afghanistan and brought back opium to Pakistan" (Chouvy 2004, 2).

Over the next ten years, the Taliban nearly tripled the opium production, from 34,000 hectares in 1989 to 91,000 hectares in 1999. During this time, al Qaeda leadership and training camps became intertwined with the Taliban, a link that proved to be one of the principal reasons for the US-led invasion of Afghanistan following the al Qaeda attack against the US on 11 September 2001. While the Afghan al Qaeda training camps have been destroyed, coalition forces continue to engage al Qaeda and Taliban forces in Afghanistan and opium production continues at a rate higher than when the Taliban governed the country. In recognition of this fact, the US has implemented a combined task force to assist the Afghan government in its eradication efforts.

In March 2005, six DEA officers and thirty-six Afghan narcotics policemen conducted raids in Nangahar Province while the US military provided transportation and security. Along with the active DEA participation, the Department of State (DOS) is coordinating other eradication efforts with the Afghan government. Also, Great Britain is now commanding the CN mission in Afghanistan. Nevertheless, is the US missing the mark?

With 20,000 US troops operating in Afghanistan, are there assets already in place to counter the opium financing of terrorism? "Under previous guidelines . . . American troops were authorized to seize or destroy drugs and drug equipment only if they came across them in the course of traditional military activities to capture or kill insurgents and terrorists. . . . Under the new mission guidance, the Department of Defense will provide 'transportation, planning assistance, intelligence, targeting packages' to the counter narcotics mission, said one senior Pentagon official" (Shanker 2005, 2). Is this new mission guidance enough?

US Army SF have long been actively involved in CN missions. In fact, CN activities have been part of SF doctrine for years under the overarching mission of collateral activities. Given the scope of the Department of Defense's (DOD) CN policy and Army doctrine, SF commanders should evaluate increasing SOF integration into the coalition's CN efforts to eliminate the illicit drug funding of terrorist organizations in support of the broader GWOT.

Definitions

Counterdrug (CD) versus Counternarcotics: It should be noted that within the scope of this study the terms CD and CN are the same. The joint publication (JP) concerning counterdrug operations, JP 3-07.4, *Joint Counterdrug Operations*, 17 February 1998, makes no mention of the term CN. However, many of the sources researched for this study made no distinction between the two terms. Within this study CN will be used except when matching the context of the individual source being analyzed. Within DOD's description of its CN policy it uses the definition, "Those measures taken to detect, interdict, disrupt, or curtail any activity that is reasonably related to narcotics trafficking. This includes, but is not limited to, measures taken to detect, interdict, disrupt, or curtail activities related to substances, materiel, weapons, or resources used to finance, support, secure, cultivate, process, or transport illegal drugs" (DOD 2002).

Counterdrug activities: According to the US Army's Field Manual 3-05.20, *Special Forces Operations*, CD activities are defined as "Measures taken to detect, monitor, and counter the production, trafficking, and use of illegal drugs" (2001, 2-22).

Hectares: A metric unit of measure, equal to 100 ares (2.471 acres or 10,000 square meters).

Interagency Coordination: DOD JP 1-02 defines IA coordination as: "Within the context of Department of Defense involvement, the coordination that occurs between elements of Department of Defense, and engaged US Government agencies, nongovernmental organizations, and regional and international organizations for the purpose of accomplishing an objective" (2005, 269).

Special Forces: "US Army forces organized, trained, and equipped to conduct special operations with an emphasis on unconventional warfare capabilities" (JP 2005, 495).

Special Operations: Operations conducted in hostile, denied, or politically sensitive environments to achieve military, diplomatic, informational, and/or economic objectives employing military capabilities for which there is no broad conventional force requirement. These operations often require covert, clandestine, or low visibility capabilities. Special operations are applicable across the range of military operations. They can be conducted independently or in conjunction with operations of conventional forces or other government agencies and may include operations through, with, or by indigenous or surrogate forces. Special operations differ from conventional operations in degree of physical and political risk, operational techniques, mode of employment, independence from friendly support, and dependence on detailed operational intelligence and indigenous assets. (JP 2005, 496).

Assumptions

The underlying assumption in this project is that terrorist organizations like al Qaeda are using the profits from narcotrafficking to fund their terrorist operations. There is strong evidence to support this theory, evidence that will be addressed in greater detail in the analysis portion of this project. US government officials, international organizations, and private citizens who have studied this topic all have reached the conclusion that terrorists are indeed linked to the Afghan opium trade. Therefore, following a background portion of the topic in the following chapters to inform the reader on various opinions, the thesis will then discuss current measures being taken to combat the problem, a historical model of what has been successful in the past, and then recommendation for further action.

Limitations

One of the limitations of this study is that beginning in April 2006, German forces will assume command of the International Security Assistance Force in Afghanistan. Commensurate with this is an expected US military reduction in force. This thesis is written from the perspective that this has not happened yet and that US conventional forces and SF are still operating in relatively large numbers in Afghanistan. This is a limitation in that if US military forces are to be used as a component of an overall CN solution, then this may not be feasible once a reduction in force happens. Another limitation is the research cutoff for this project, which was 31 December 2005.

Delimitations

All information gathered and written is from open source documents and therefore unclassified. Additionally, no discussion will be made here regarding US Title 10 and 50 authority and responsibilities. This delimitation is being imposed since an entire thesis can be dedicated to this issue alone, and therefore no attempt will be made to comprehensively address this. Should any recommendations here cloud the line between US law, the recommendation would be to introduce legislation similar to the Goldwater-Nichols Act to address these issues.

Also, given the underlying assumption of this thesis that there is indeed a link between narcotrafficking and al Qaeda, a comprehensive review of law enforcement data concerning this economic link was specifically omitted from the scope of the research due to the broad range of multiple reputable sources who agree that this nexus exists.

Significance of the Study

One significance of this study is the fact that traditional methods of engaging and destroying the enemy are nearly worthless against an elusive opponent. Given that terrorist organizations are becoming increasingly difficult to target using lethal means, new methods of disrupting their networks should be employed. Eliminating their financial support from illicit drugs can be one of those methods. While conventional forces are engaged in the tactical fight against enemy forces in Iraq and Afghanistan, al Qaeda retains the ability to fund global operations through the revenue generated from narcotrafficking in Afghanistan. While this is not the only source of funding, it is one source that the US military can interdict while conducting operations in Afghanistan. Tactical commanders of all branches and services need to understand that by not actively addressing this issue within their area of influence they are in some manner abetting the enemy. An additional hope of this thesis is to educate commanders about the problem of narcotrafficking as a source of funding for al Qaeda and provide recommendations as to what can be done without targeting local farmers, who are merely trying to survive, and alienating citizens from the fledgling government trying to eradicate poppy crops.

Additionally, commanders such as Supreme Allied Commander, Europe, and Commander of the United States European Command, General James Jones, and politicians, such as US Representative Mark Steven Kirk, recognize the alarming importance of tackling this problem. In 2004, Kirk remarked about the clear connection between narcotrafficking and al Qaeda. In fact, he maintains it is their number one source of financing for their terrorist operations (Scarborough 2004, 1). In 2005, Jones stated that the opium trade is "the number one problem that Afghanistan has to face for its future" (2005, 6). These are not just the remarks of a few men, but rather the remarks of two key US leaders in a series of articles and statements that suggest the magnitude of the problem. And while the US has dedicated partners in Afghanistan and in the GWOT, the US is in a unique position to bring to bear all instruments of national power--diplomatic, informational, military, and economic means--to fight the issue of drugs. Only by attacking the problem from all of these directions might the solution be found.

Finally, and of additional significance, is that if as a part of researching this thesis a plausible model can be identified and employed to interdict the funding of terrorist organizations through narcotrafficking, the US can make use of the model in other areas of operations in the GWOT.

CHAPTER 2

LITERATURE REVIEW AND METHODOLOGY

Literature Review

Many books have been written on narcoterrorism, most of them centering on the

FARC and Colombia. However, the FARC is not as prolific a global influence as the

predominant terrorist organization in Afghanistan, al Qaeda. Therefore, not all of the

models suggested in these writings are particularly applicable to this study. Since

relatively few authors until 11 September 2001 dedicated writing time to the connection

between Afghan opium production and the funding of terrorist organizations, a majority

of the research material for this study will be online research. Several US Army War

College Strategy Research Projects have been helpful in focusing this study, as have

UNODC, DEA, and Senate reports, projects, and summaries which are available online.

Multiple online news services have also been beneficial. The US Army online Doctrine

Library was also used in the initial research. With the exception of the statistics-heavy

UNODC report, all of the research material has pointed to the direct, albeit covert,

connection between illicit drugs and the funding of terrorist organizations. A vast

majority of the materials make an effort to point out the need to do more and to do it

quickly.

Many sources fault the US government for not acting quicker, but all argue that

sufficient forces should be used, as long as they are there, to eradicate Afghan opium.

Several sources argue the US assumed the responsibility to eradicate opium production

when it invaded; they contend it is a moral responsibility now. In particular, testimony by

Robert Perito, Special Advisor for the Rule of Law Program for the United States

Institute of Peace, before the Senate Foreign Relations Committee is prominent. He stated, "The US-led Coalition and the International Security Assistance Force (ISAF) must actively assist in the fight against narcotics. . . . Military forces must begin pro-actively performing at least a limited number of counter narcotic enforcement functions . . . (in order to) help correct the misimpression of Afghans that the US military condones participation of warlords in the drug trade" (2005, 6).

Some other examples from the numerous news articles from sources such as *The Washington Times*, *Time* magazine, and *USA Today* have addressed the funding of al Qaeda and other terrorist organizations through the trafficking of narcotics. However, these are more difficult to vet, due to the prolific use of unnamed sources and lack of attributable material, but will be used when varying sources, albeit unnamed, reach the same conclusion. Furthermore, these articles tend to sensationalize certain aspects of the story, providing a mere snapshot of one operation or investigation.

One example can be found in a *Time* magazine article written by Elaine Shannon. "Although Afghanistan's poppy farmers produce about 87% of the world's opium, according to a recent United Nations report, the Bush Administration has been unwilling to deploy the U.S. military to eradicate poppy fields for fear of antagonizing the hundreds of thousands of impoverished villagers whose livelihoods depend on the crop" (2005, 1). While the premise of this thesis is that active disrupting of narcotrafficking in Afghanistan by any agency would directly contribute to the GWOT, Shannon's statement fails to provide the reader the full picture. Crop eradication has never been the purview of the US military, and it is, in fact, taking place under the supervision of the Afghan government with support from advisors from the DEA, the UNODC, and OGAs. To say

13

that the narcotrafficking problem exists because of the administration's failure "to deploy the U.S. military to eradicate poppy fields" (2005, 1) is misleading because this is a DEA mission.

In *Time Asia* magazine, Tim McGirk wrote an article titled "Terrorism's Harvest," with reporting by Elaine Shannon, in the 2 August 2004 edition. Shannon's help seems to show through as McGirk writes, "For their part, U.S. military commanders have been reluctant to commit the nearly 20,000 U.S. troops in Afghanistan to opium eradication. . . . But the U.S. is finally starting to pay attention" (2004, 2). Again, the choice of words and the context in which they are presented suggests a reporting bias in the weekly which one would associate with an editorial column, somewhat limiting its application. That said, where direct quotes are attributed and statistics given they will be included in this analysis where applicable.

The Washington Times article "Heroin Traffic Finances bin Laden" is a helpful example of direct quotations. In the 6 December 2004 article by Rowan Scarborough, Illinois Representative Mark Kirk is reported to have said, "We now know al Qaeda's dominant source of funding is the illegal sale of narcotics" (2004, 1). Kirk is paraphrased when the author of the article states that "bin Laden's al Qaeda terror organization is reaping $28 million a year in illicit heroin sales" (2004, 1). Given the contentious nature of this issue, all sources reflect the author's bias to a varying degree. In order to limit this bias multiple sources will be used throughout the thesis.

Up to this point the primary research material has been, "The Emerging Threat of Illicit Drug Funding of Terrorist Organizations," by LTC Jackie L. Reaves, AV, published as a US Army War College Strategy Research Project. While the majority of the paper seems to be a patchwork of quotations from various sources, they transition well together and, more importantly, the bibliography has a wealth of resources on which to follow up. The Reaves project is relatively free from bias and appears to have no motivation other than to present the link between terrorist organizations and narcotrafficking. Her project is divided into three main points: the financial sustainment of terrorist organizations, the viability of illicit drugs as a weapon of mass destruction, and the potential of illicit drugs to impair the readiness of US armed forces. While this last topic is supported by statistical data from Vietnam and other historical references, it is beyond the scope of this thesis and will not be addressed further. The project sources many helpful documents in the bibliography that have proved useful in this thesis research.

The UNODC web site has provided the backbone for the statistical data incorporated in this thesis. Unbiased, the *Summary Findings of Opium Trends in Afghanistan, 2005*, dated 12 September 2005, is an excellent source for data concerning amounts of opium being harvested, regional breakdowns of opium harvesting, and the historical data to support trend analysis of this topic. The summary also graphically identifies, by province, government programs, both Afghan-led eradication and alternative livelihood (AL) commitment in US dollars. This information is then shown three different ways: historical and current opium cultivation, and opium cultivation change. It is easy to compare the maps to conclude that the areas receiving the lowest eradication efforts and monetary commitment are the areas which have seen the greatest rise in opium cultivation. The summary also charts the price of opium, the number of farmers harvesting opium, and the percentage of Afghan gross domestic product opium provides to the country.

The UNODC web site also lists the current projects underway addressing the CN issues. These programs are merely factual listings of what governments and agencies are involved, how they are specifically arrayed, and in what capacity. The UNODC is listed as the lead agency in the institutional development of Kabul's CND. The programs range from drug-related law enforcement training, led by the United Kingdom (UK), to Iran's support to work with the UNODC in the area of border control, to internal efforts to combat drug abuse with support from Canada, Ireland, and Italy.

US government web sites were used to determine what agencies were involved, their task organization, and the chain of command. The *Joint Force Quarterly* provided the information concerning the formation of the Joint IA Task Force – Counterterrorism. This task force brought together subject matter experts "from the Federal Bureau of Investigation (FBI), Central Intelligence Agency (CIA), Diplomatic Security Services, Customs Service, National Security Agency, Defense Intelligence Agency, Defense Human Intelligence Agency, New York's Joint Terrorism Task Force, and the Justice, Treasury, and State Departments, among others" (Bogdanos 2005, 2). This author provided factual examples of the methods and organizations being used in the CN role in Afghanistan. He concluded with recommendations for further actions, which can be categorized as opinion, but which are tied closely with observations of these activities.

The US Library of Congress link to the Congressional Research Service (CRS) provided background through the RL 32686 report, *Afghanistan: Narcotics and U.S. Policy*. No bias was indicated, and the report provided a wealth of information concerning US involvement in Afghan CN activities. Of note was the subparagraph "Narcotics, Insurgency and Terrorism," which draws the link between narcotics trafficking and the financing of terrorist organizations. Additionally, later subjects include "Defining the Role of the U.S. Military" and "U.S. Policy Initiatives." The report paraphrases the Defense Department response to the CRS inquiry: "U.S. Military forces in Afghanistan will not directly target drug production facilities or pursue drug traffickers as part of the new U.S. initiative. Current rules of engagement allow U.S. forces to seize and destroy drugs and drug infrastructure discovered during the course of military operations" (CRS 2005, 32).

The Afghan government web site for the CND of the National Security Council and Ministry of Rural Rehabilitation and Development was researched to determine what steps are being taken to address the National Drug Control Strategy (NDCS). The web site addresses US Security Council resolution 1378 of 14 November 2001, which states the Afghan Government "should respect Afghanistan's international obligations, including cooperating fully in international efforts to combat terrorism and illicit drug trafficking within and from Afghanistan" (CND 2005, 1). The NDCS lays out the key elements of the program and the specific objectives needed to accomplish the goals.

The DOD publication *Military Review* solicits articles from DOD personnel in order to disseminate thoughts from the field. One article, "Drug Wars, Counterinsurgency, and the National Guard," written by Major Reyes Z. Cole, suggests increasing the cooperation of the National Guard Counterdrug Support Program (NGCDSP) in regional CN operations such as Afghanistan. Cole suggests that the CN missions conducted by National Guard soldiers in the US should be used to assist other agencies in the CN fight. He links the similarities between CN and counterinsurgency (COIN) operations through three NGCDSP characteristics: specialized training, practical field experience, and a joint, IA problem-solving mindset. His thoughts are well connected and presented in a factual manner. Any pervasive bias is not noticeable. Many of his facts relate to a US territorial model, such as his emphasis on the 1989 National Defense Authorization Act, which "identifies drugs as a clear present threat to U.S. security and designates the Department of Defense (DOD) as the lead agency to detect and monitor drug shipments into the country" (Cole 2005, 70). However, this continental-US-centric thought serves as a backbone for his article and does not detract from his final recommendation, "The NGCDSP can support COIN operations overseas . . . with emphasis on matters related to coca and poppy cultivation" (Cole 2005, 73).

Other *Military Review* articles that have proved useful are from the March 1990 issue. Two articles discuss the US military CN role in South America, in particular Colombia, Bolivia and Peru. The articles are "Narcoterrorism: The New Unconventional War" by Major Mark Hertling, and "Andean Drug Trafficking and the Military Option" by Donald Mabry. These articles, while essentially editorial suggestions on the part of an Army officer and a Senior Fellow in the Center for International Security and Strategic Studies respectively, are factual and relatively unbiased. Both articles provide a succinct case study on the South American "War on Drugs."

Mark Bowden's nonfiction study of the Colombian cocaine problem, *Killing Pablo*, was also helpful in researching the US military's role in Latin American CN operations. Bowden's background as an investigative reporter for the *Philadelphia Enquirer* is readily apparent by his extensive research into the history and tactics employed in the book. There is no evidence that any of the facts portrayed in the book are false.

Methodology

The methodology components used to answer the research questions are as follows; terrorism and Afghan opium, the Afghan opium problem, the US military's role in CN operations, a SOF CN case study, the warlord problem, IA coordination in Afghanistan, and beyond the IA approach. Through the analysis of these components it is possible to answer the primary question and conclude whether or not the current IA CN strategy is able to have an impact on Afghanistan's opium dependency opium.

Before any attempt at answering the primary research question, it was important to establish the link between terrorism, specifically its link to al Qaeda, and Afghan opium. Since no quantitative analysis can be made concerning this link, the topic will be addressed through the subjective analysis from multiple reputable sources. As noted in the assumption and delimitation portion of this project, no attempt was made to audit economic data concerning the connection between narcotrafficking and al Qaeda. The plethora of statements, testimonies, and circumstantial evidence is discussed in the section covering terrorism and Afghan opium. This material will be used to show the extent of US involvement in Afghanistan's CN program, what IA coordination is being done, and whether this assistance is effective, thus helping to answer the primary research question.

Following this is a quantitative analysis of Afghan opium production and cultivation in order to address the fact that opium production and trafficking in Afghanistan is an extremely pervasive problem that has a significant corrosive effect in

19

the establishment of the new Afghan government. This aspect is detailed in the UNODC statistical data provided in the beginning of the analysis chapter.

After discussing the opium problem and its link with terrorist organizations, a background of US military support to CN operations is provided in both the context of the current operating environment and a historical model. The model is being used to show US successes in using the military in CN operations, and should be recognized as important to answering the secondary question in this thesis. This case study will focus on US military efforts in Latin America beginning in the 1980s and continuing today. In particular, the employment of SF in Bolivia, Colombia, and Peru will be highlighted in order to support the later discussion on the use of SF in Afghanistan. This topic is brought full circle back to the current Afghan opium problem with an explanation of one of the major road blocks the Afghan CN fight: warlordism. This aspect of Afghan culture ties back into the US military's effort to destroy al Qaeda and the Taliban by, with, and through Afghan militias. However, the military's support of warlords makes the Afghan opium problem more difficult, as many warlords were involved in narcotrafficking. SF teams assisting warlords in the fight against the Taliban in 2001-2002 were directed to terminate their assistance if they had reason to believe the warlords were still engaged in narcotrafficking. So while some warlords continue their narcotrafficking operations the military does not condone this and does not work with those warlords.

With this background established, the thesis follows with a look at the current IA coordination as it pertains to Afghan CN operations. Central to the IA coordination is the DOS "five-pillars" model, which addresses law enforcement, interdiction, eradication, AL, and public information. It is through this approach that it is then possible to address the research questions. Once the current parameters are known it is then possible to look at the statistical data provided by the UNODC to see if there are indeed appropriate measures being taken to disrupt the opium trade in Afghanistan and therefore deprive al Qaeda a major source of funding for its operations. Once this is done, this project will look at how the military fits into Afghan CN operations and whether SOF can provide greater assistance.

The strength of this approach is that a comprehensive picture of the problem of Afghanistan is presented and put into the context of the larger picture. No CN operations can be undertaken by the military without affecting the other aspects presented, whether Afghan culture, foreign assistance, or other military operations.

Therefore, through the methodology of analyzing each of these components – terrorism and Afghan opium, the Afghan opium problem, the US military's role in CN operations, a SOF CN case study, the warlord problem, IA coordination in Afghanistan, and beyond the five-pillars approach – a complete model of the Afghan CN strategy is formed. Through the analysis of these aspects, and with quantitative support from the UNODC report, it is possible to conclude whether or not the current IA CN structure is effective.

CHAPTER 3

ANALYSIS

Afghanistan eclipses the next largest global supplier of opium by a factor of ten.

Afghanistan produced 4200 metric tons of opium in 2005 and Myanmar produced 370

metric tons (UNODC WDR 2005, 177). The UNODC estimated that in 2005, the country

would export 2.7 billion dollars worth of opium beyond its borders (UNODC 2005, 1).

This figure represents 52 percent of Afghanistan's gross domestic product. If anything

positive can be seen in these data it is a slight improvement over the 2004 statistics. That

year saw 2.8 billion dollars, representing 61 percent of the national gross domestic

product. The street value of this quantity of opium product is estimated at thirty-six

billion dollars. The fact that al Qaeda is profiting from narcotrafficking and funding its

global operations through part of these proceeds (see below) indicates that this is an

international problem that goes well beyond the responsibility and, more to the point,

capability of the fledgling government of Kabul.

Afghan President Hamid Karzai fully recognizes the immense problem in

Afghanistan and is welcoming international support to stop the exploding opium trade

within his borders. Following an attack that left nearly twenty policemen dead in October

2005, Karzai suggested there was "cooperation between the drug trade and terrorism"

(USA Today 2005). To help eradicate the growing opium problem in Afghanistan,

Karzai's government created the CND within the National Security Council in 2002 as

the key policy-coordinating agency for domestic CN operations. According to

Afghanistan Transitional Authority documents, the CND has developed a ten-year plan called the, NDCS.

The NDCS has five elements: First, "The provision of alternative livelihoods for Afghan poppy farmer; (Second,) The extension of drug law enforcement throughout Afghanistan; (Third,) The implementation of drug control legislation; (Fourth,) The establishment of effective institutions; (Fifth,) The introduction and prevention of treatment programmes for addicts" (NDCS 2003, 2). This agency coordinates its activities with the coalition Counter-Narcotics Working Group, comprised of representatives from the US, Britain, Afghanistan, and Pakistan. Currently, the British forces head the Counter-Narcotics Working Group. Specific military coordination is made through the Joint Interagency Task Force - Counterterrorism.

The United Nations has widely documented the growing problem in opium production, tracking opium harvest data for years. Afghanistan supplies 87 percent of the world's opium, and globally has been the largest heroin supplier for nearly two decades.

Terrorism and Afghan Opium

Congressional documents suggest the importance of CN programs. In the CRS report for the 109th Congress one of the key sections, the "Situation in Afghanistan" portion, directly addresses the link between narcotrafficking and the funding of terrorist organizations.

> U.S. officials have expressed concern that Taliban insurgents, Al Qaeda operatives, and associated regional terrorists organizations are profiting from and consolidating the illegal cultivation and trafficking of opium and heroin in Afghanistan, with an associated increase in corruption of regional and local officials. . . . Administration officials have placed renewed emphasis on counter-narcotics as a key component of U.S. efforts in Afghanistan. On November 17, 2004, the State Department announced the interagency "Plan Afghanistan"

initiative, which will redouble U.S. counternarcotics efforts in Afghanistan through public-awareness outreach, judicial reform, alternative development programs, interdiction, and a broad opium poppy eradication campaign. (2004, 6)

Robert M. Perito of the United States Institute of Peace testified before the Senate Foreign Relations Committee in May 2004 on the opium problem in Afghanistan. He points out that "Profits from narcotics trafficking also find their way through supporters to the Taliban and al Qaeda and are used to finance local and international terrorism" (2004, 2).

US Representative Mark Steven Kirk (IL-R) could not agree more. Says Kirk, "We now know al Qaeda's dominant source of funding is the illegal sale of narcotics" (Scarborough 2004, 1). Kirk sponsored legislation in 2004 authorizing the DOS to pay cash rewards, or their equivalent, for information about drug lords and their activities.

While nearly impossible to prove, Indian intelligence suggests that Osama bin Laden once controlled sixty heroin laboratories, the profits from which he used to finance his terrorist operations (Olcott and Udalova 2000, 24). Ali Abul Nazzar, once close to bin Laden and now in US custody, said of bin Laden's funding, "The money comes from heroin, not from (bin Laden's father's) personal holdings" (Blanchfield 2002). Bin Laden spent the better part of six years in Afghanistan supporting the Taliban with profits from heroin trafficking approaching one billion dollars annually. It was during this period that bin Laden's al Qaeda network branched out, becoming the most widely known global terrorist organization today. After the US-led invasion of Afghanistan, bin Laden was forced into hiding, most likely in the mountainous border region between Afghanistan and Pakistan. The invasion may have impacted al Qaeda's funding inadvertently due to the significant drop in harvested opium in 2001-2002. This drop has been attributed to

24

farmers' fear of getting caught growing what they know is an illegal crop by US troops

and also the disruption of traffickers' ability to easily operate during the peak of the war.

Once farmers realized that neither the US military nor the interim Afghan government

was focused on opium crops, opium cultivation increased dramatically, as seen in the

2003-2005 data. Additionally, since the US focus remained on capturing and killing

terrorists, traffickers regained momentum and renewed their vigor in capitalizing on the

revitalized opium industry.

The Afghan Opium Problem

The following discussion further illustrates the enormity of the opium problem in

Afghanistan. The UNODC has been keeping detailed analysis of worldwide opium

production since 1990. In that year, Myanmar and Afghanistan each produced 1600

metric tons, for a total of 84 percent of the world-wide opium market. (Worldwide opium

production data are graphically represented within the UNODC report and figures are

rounded to the nearest hundred metric tons.) The Lao People's Democratic Republic

produced 200 metric tons, or roughly 5 percent of worldwide totals, and the remaining

400 metric tons, or 11 percent, were produced in the rest of the world. Total global

production in 1990 was 3800 metric tons. Myanmar continued to produce roughly 1600

metric tons until 2002, when tonnage began to decrease each year to approximately 300

metric tons in 2005. Data for the Lao People's Democratic Republic also remained

relatively static until 2004, when opium production was cut in half, and in 2005 opium

production was completely eliminated through government eradication and law

enforcement efforts. Similarly, the rest of the world production rates remain relatively static, plus or minus one hundred metric tons, throughout the entire timeframe (UNODC 2005, 7).

Only in Afghanistan do opium production rates increase dramatically. By 1994, opium production rates had more than doubled to 3400 metric tons, and by 1999 production climbed to 4600 metric tons, the highest rate to date. This is the same year the Taliban solidified control of all but the outermost provinces in Afghanistan. Only in 2001 did production drop 1600 metric tons to an insignificant 200 metric tons. Unfortunately, 2002 witnessed an increase over the 2000 production, rising back to 3400 metric tons, making Afghanistan once again the leading global supplier of opium. While 2005 saw the global opium production level down 19 percent from an all time high of 5800 metric tons in 1999, Afghanistan provided a staggering 87 percent of the global supply. However, this equates to 4100 metric tons from Afghanistan, reflecting a marginal decrease from 4200 metric tons in 2004. Thus, despite this decrease, Afghan opium-production remains an exponentially more significant global supplier than all other opium producing nations in the entire world. Additionally, despite the global decrease in production, Afghanistan opium production remains near an all time high, despite Afghan government programs, US IA efforts, and coalition assistance in combating the enormous problem (UNODC 2005, 7).

Next, the UNODC findings discuss eradication efforts. Through a variety of programs, led by provincial governors, eradication of opium poppy amounted to approximately 5100 hectares, or about 5 percent of the 2005 Afghan opium cultivation. This effort was assisted by the central government's augmentation of the Central Poppy Eradication Force (CPEF) and the Afghan National Police. The largest eradication efforts were taken in Nangarhar and Hilmand province, the two largest producing provinces in Afghanistan, and were conducted almost exclusively by the provincial governors. Eradication resulted in 46 percent and 26 percent decreases in these areas respectively (UNODC, 2005, 9).

The UNODC findings point out a discrepancy in the numbers reported by the provincial governors to the Ministry of Interior and those verified by the UNODC. The governors reported a total eradication figure of 36,408 hectares, some 19,000 hectares in the Uruzgan province alone. The UNODC suggests the reporting problem exists because "several governors were overly optimistic with regard to the success of their eradication efforts" (UNODC 2005, 10). However, the report continues, "irrespective of these data discrepancies, the threat of large-scale eradication appears to have played a significant role in farmers' decisions not to plant opium poppy in 2005" (UNODC 2005, 10).

The UNODC also surveyed farmers in an effort to elicit their reasons for either reducing or increasing cultivation in 2005. The survey included 2064 farmers in 1180 Afghan villages. Seventy percent of farmers responded that the single largest reason for them to decrease opium poppy cultivation was the fear of eradication. The next highest reported reason at 40 percent was the fear of imprisonment. The only remaining reason higher than 10 percent was cited as religious reasons, that is, 32 percent reported they decreased cultivation because it was banned by Islam, a problem the Taliban ignored when it suited their own needs. Of those who increased cultivation in 2005, 42 percent stated it was because of high opium prices. Twenty-four percent of respondents said that higher demand from traffickers was a reason they increased cultivation. Additionally, 42 percent of farmers stated they increased cultivation due to an increase in the cost of consumer goods, and 26 percent noted the high cost of weddings. These last two reasons suggest an inflationary pressure that the central government will need to address as part of a holistic approach to the opium problem (UNODC 2005, 11-12).

The UNODC findings continue with a review of the AL programs ongoing in Afghanistan as a part of the NDCS. The overarching AL program is a ten-year, 1.2-billion-dollar program to encourage farmers to grow anything other than opium poppies. The data are discussed in terms of the Islamic calendar year 1384, which divides the Christian calendar years of 2005 and 2006, but still represents approximately one fiscal year in the US. Total funds committed for 2005/2006 are 490 million dollars, with 41 percent of those funds going to the Nangarhar, Hilmand, Badakshan and Uruzgan provinces. Of the total thirty-two Afghan provinces, these four provinces accounted for some 64 percent of the 2004 Afghan opium cultivation and were the only provinces to report opium cultivation measured above 10,000 ha. The next highest province cultivated 4,983 hectares in 2004. Unfortunately, while eradication and AL programs seem to have reduced the four leading provinces to only 38 percent of the total Afghan cultivation, three other provinces, Bakh, Farah, and Kandahar, saw a threefold increase, and Hilmand only saw a marginal drop from 29,353 hectares in 2004 to 26,500 hectares in 2005. Hilmand retains the highest opium cultivation rate in the entire country, despite a 21 percent decrease in overall Afghan cultivation (UNODC 2005, 4).

Suggesting an increase in the effectiveness of the central government, the largest decreases in cultivation from 2004 to 2005 were in the provinces surrounding Kabul province. Every province bordering Kabul province showed a strong decrease in cultivation, anywhere between a 50 to 100 percent decrease. Neighboring Nangarhar, reported a hopeful 96 percent decrease. Nearby Badakhshan reported a 53 percent decrease. Three of the four provinces reporting the strongest increase are also three of the most remote provinces, although one of these provinces, Kandahar, might represent a different aspect of government control. The decrease may not be due to the physical distance from the central government, but rather its proximity to radical Islamic militants in Pakistan and the resurgence of Taliban extremists (UNODC 2005, 23-24).

Concerning the breakdown of total committed AL funds for 2005/2006, it is perhaps worthy to note that the US, through the US Agency for International Development (USAID), is the largest single nation donor to the AL program, with 154 million dollars committed. The World Bank has committed the slightly higher amount of 158 million dollars. The UK has committed 67 million dollars, and the European Commission 41 million dollars (UNODC 2005, 14).

The US Military's Role in CN Operations

Unfortunately, the UNODC estimates that 2005 will be the highest yielding opium harvest since 1999, at over 3,600 tons, or roughly $36 billion in street value. While al Qaeda may not be directly tied to the harvesting and production anymore, they are by all accounts involved in the trafficking portion of the opium trade. This is where the highest profits are. By supplying the protection for labs and convoys, al Qaeda receives substantial cuts of the profits. *Time* magazine reported on the connection by reporting about a US Navy ship searching a boat in the Arabian Sea: "says a Western antinarcotics official, 'they found several al-Qaeda guys sitting on a bale of drugs'" (McGirk 2004, 2). In another example from *Time*, when coalition CN agents raided a house in Kabul, over ten satellite phones were found, and when checked, the phones "had been used to call suspected terrorists in Turkey, the Balkans and Western Europe" (McGirk 2004, 2).

Administration officials are naturally hesitant to turn any military attention away from the clear military objectives. No one in the current administration wants to be blamed for a Somalia-like "mission creep," where the US military mission grew ambiguous over time. Mission creep is the shifting of efforts away from the original task and the detraction from mission accomplishment. To the point, Secretary of Defense Donald Rumsfeld stated he does not want the "Over-stretched 8,000 US soldiers in Afghanistan to become sidetracked from their main goal: to capture and kill terrorists. And chasing drug smugglers could take away allies from the Americans" (McGirk 2003, 23). Tim McGirk of *Time* magazine painted a slightly different picture when he wrote of soldiers being told to ignore a convoy of opium traffickers. "Afghan officials say that several times last year U.S. special forces spotted suspicious convoys that appeared to be ferrying opium. Radioing in for order, the special forces were told to leave the convoys alone and keep hunting for al Qaeda. . . . A senior Afghan security official says the U.S. military doesn't want to jeopardize the help it receives from local commanders by seizing drug stashes or busting labs controlled by friendly warlords" (McGirk 2004, 2).

CN operations are not a new paradigm for the military. In 1991, then Chairman of the Joint Chiefs of Staff General Colin Powell testified before the Senate Committee on Armed Services that "the detection and countering of the production and trafficking of illegal drugs is a high-priority national security mission of our armed forces" (1991, 27). At this time, cocaine represented the gravest threat to national security from the perspective of the continuing "War on Drugs." The year Powell made his remarks to the

House marked the fifth anniversary of Operation Blast Furnace, in which US military personnel led CN missions in Bolivia in an effort to attack the supply side of illegal coca production. In the March 1990 issue of *Military Review*, Major Mark Hertling wrote, "While the *tactical* phase of the operation was reported to be a success – during the four months the operation took place, the cocaine industry in Bolivia was essentially paralyzed – the *operational* aspect of the campaign was lacking" (Hertling 1990, 22). All of this leads to a possible model for today's problem of illicit funding of terrorist organizations.

By taking a quick survey of the multidecade effort to combat the Latin American cocaine crisis one can better understand how this translates into the CN operations of today. The military played a decreasing role after Operation Blast Furnace; however, US SF provided a large percentage of these forces. SF bring a unique characteristic to austere environments such as Latin America in the 1980s and 1990s and Afghanistan today. All SF soldiers are required to speak a second language and SF units are regionally oriented in order to maximize their soldiers' cultural understanding. Coupling these elements with the SF charter of working by, with, or through indigenous forces, SF works as a force multiplier – organizing foreign forces to do what would take battalions of US conventional forces to do.

SOF Case Study: Latin America

Operation Blast Furnace represented a turning point in US policy. For the first time in modern history the US was actively pursuing an aggressive CN policy outside of its own borders. The Bolivian operation was an extension of President Reagan's April 1986 "classified National Security Decision Directive that declared the flow of drugs across U.S. borders to be a 'national security threat'" (Bowden 2001, 64). While First Lady Nancy Reagan was addressing the demand side of the drug problem by going to the airwaves and telling the public to "Just Say No," the US military was inserting soldiers into the Bolivian jungles to destroy coca crops and production labs. Bolivia was key in the war on drugs, as it, Colombia, and Peru did, and continue to, produce roughly 97 percent of the global coca product. As Hertling suggested, the tactical portion of the military action seemed to be a success, as measured by the near elimination of exported Bolivian coca (Christian 1986, 1). However, the US failed to apply all the instruments of national power by not equally supporting the diplomatic, information, and economic lines of operation. Failure to assist local law enforcement agencies, the Bolivian justice system, and its own military merely caused a temporary halt in coca exportation. When the US military ceased its offensive operations and began training the Bolivian Army to take over, coca production once again soared back to life at its pre-Blast Furnace level.

In 1989 President George H. W. Bush attempted to pursue an even more comprehensive approach than his predecessor had. On 21 August 1989 he signed National Security Directive 18, an IA approach, allocating more than 250 million dollars worth of assistance in the form of military, law enforcement, and intelligence assets as part of his Andean Initiative (Bowden 2001, 64). The directive states, "These programs will involve expanded assistance to indigenous police, military, and intelligence officials in all three countries, for the purpose of assisting them to regain control of their countries from an insidious combination of insurgent and drug traffickers and to suppress the flow of narcotics to the United States" (Bush 1989, 2). Additionally, "A week later he authorized another $65 million in emergency military aid to Colombia alone, and he authorized sending a small number of U.S. Special Forces troops to Colombia to train its police and military in rapid-strike tactics" (Bowden 2001, 65).

SF soldiers are uniquely qualified to conduct such operations. Due to the nature of their organization, SF soldiers are more senior in rank than conventional forces. This, combined with their comparatively larger portion of DOD's budget, allows them to be better trained and equipped than their conventional force counterparts. Due to these special qualifications SF units are specifically trained to conduct CN operations, as summed up within the excerpt from SF doctrine that follows.

> Using their skills in cross-cultural communications, SF personnel train HN (Host Nation) CD forces on critical skills required to conduct small-unit CD operations. . . . Although some CD activities can be classified FID (Foreign Internal Defense), most are undertaken as part of legislatively authorized and specifically funded U.S. CD programs, rather than as participation in another government's program to combat this lawlessness. These U.S. CD programs may be multinational or conducted in DS (Direct Support) of HN efforts. (FM 3-05.20 2001, 2-22)

Given President Bush's emphasis on his Andean Initiative, it should not be surprising that "the newly appointed drug czar, William J. Bennett, had all but advocated sending U.S. military hit squads to kill the infamous *narcos*" (Bowden 2001, 65). The term "narcos" comes from the Colombian colloquial phrase meaning cocaine traffickers. Bush had also asked the Department of Justice (DOJ) to work "on an opinion that would approve unilateral U.S. military action against narcos and terrorists in other countries, *with or without* the approval of host governments" (Bowden 2001, 65).

Taking a cue from Major Cole's article regarding the similarities between COIN and CN operations, one is able to see, with hindsight, that the war on drugs was never going to be a short war. Both COIN and CN operations usually take decades to produce measurable effects. Between 1990 and 2000 Bolivian coca cultivation fell from providing more than 24 percent of the global supply to less than 7 percent. Peru saw similar figures: from over 52 percent of global supply in 1990 to under 20 percent in 2000. Data for Colombia are more comprehensive. It is obvious that this drop in cultivation in Bolivia and Peru was offset by a fourfold increase in Colombia at its height in 2000. Since then, Colombia has had a 50 percent reduction in coca cultivation; while the entire market has seen a 25 percent decrease (UNODC *World Drug Report* 2005, 207).

While some may argue this is hardly success, one must agree that there has been progress after six years of coca cultivation decrease. So how did this progress evolve from what "some U.S. officials describe as a . . . narco-state" (Lister 2000, 1)? Bolivia, Colombia, and Peru are finally starting to see the results of the US assistance. As will be needed in Afghanistan, a holistic approach which began in the 1980s is paying off today. Certainly, influence from the DEA has played a large role in helping these countries develop their own capacity for countering coca trafficking. This has included training of host-nation law enforcement personnel to investigate and track down drug traffickers and drug cartels. The DOJ has lent its own assistance in capacity building as well, to ensure that once narco-criminals are apprehended they will be effectively prosecuted. For most of the 1980s and the beginning of the 1990s these criminals had little to fear from Latin American courts and prisons. Judges, fearful for their lives and those of their families, often let even the pettiest of drug couriers go free at the request of the powerful drug cartels. Those who were sentenced usually served short terms under house arrest or enforcement facilities unlike prisons for other criminals. The most infamous example of this coddling by the Colombian government is the case of the notorious narco boss, Pablo Escobar.

In 1991 Escobar's lawyers had negotiated a plea agreement in which he would surrender to Colombian officials, but he would never be submitted to extradition to face a number of drug-related charges in the US. In a display of the considerable power he held over the Colombian government, the Constitutional Assembly actually "voted to formally outlaw extradition by a vote of fifty to thirteen" (Bowden 2001, 98). Perhaps even more remarkable was the fact that Escobar was allowed to build *his own* prison. Called *La Catedral*, Escobar would successfully run his cocaine ring from inside of the compound. *La Catedral* was hardly more than a fenced in estate, complete with soccer fields, gardens and lavish living quarters. When Escobar continued to order the executions of his competitors from inside his prison, the government felt forced to crack down and he simply left the compound in 1992 before being transferred to alternate living quarters. While the fact that Escobar "volunteered" to be incarcerated in first place might seem incredulous, it does demonstrate some of the successes the Colombian government had against the drug cartels with the assistance of the US government. Escobar would be killed a little over a year later, on 2 December 1993, in a shootout with soldiers from the *Bloque de Búsqueda*, or Search Bloc (Bowden 2001, 249). Some of these successful programs continue today.

The DOS, along with the host nations and the UNODC, has been instrumental in establishing AL programs and information operations designed to dissuade coca farmers from supporting an illegal industry. These programs are long-term projects, ones that slowly grow momentum. Farmers may at first be reluctant to switch to a crop for which they will only be paid a fraction of the cost; however, when faced with the combination of efforts from all the other agencies they often make the switch instead of losing their entire crop to government-led eradication or imprisonment.

OGAs lent their own brand of expertise to the problem, but the servicemen of US Southern Command were literally on the front line of the war on drugs. US military aid has certain restrictions preventing assistance to nations with poor human rights records or ones that are deemed corrupt due to drug-related issues. For example, in 1996 and 1997, Colombia was cited by the Clinton administration for lacking CN efforts and all military aid was suspended save for the ongoing SF training missions (Priest and Farah 1998, A1). The exact type of mission the SF soldiers were conducting is known as foreign internal defense. SF soldiers instruct the host-nation soldiers on a variety of military skills, from basic infantry tactics to counterterrorism and advanced urban warfare techniques.

These ongoing missions are generally done in ninety-day rotations and take place at base camps throughout the three Latin American countries mentioned above. Colombia has been the location of the majority of training exercises due to its size and the nature of the paramilitary, drug-related insurgency. At one point, insurgents controlled nearly 50 percent of the nation, causing the internal displacement of nearly 1.5 million people (UNODC 2003, 36). Although only there to train, SF soldiers are routinely at risk from the insurgents, who have threatened to kill any soldiers they encounter. The FARC, in particular, made it publicly known they would show no distinction between Colombian government forces and US soldiers in combat, both would be killed given the opportunity. Nevertheless, over the years this partnership training has built up the Andean militaries into professional armed forces capable of fighting their own internal counterinsurgencies. Through the use of a small number of SF teams operating alongside

36

their counterparts, the Andean countries are reclaiming their territories from these insurgents.

Through training exercises, SF soldiers are increasing the professionalism of the host-nation militaries. Colombia, the Western Hemisphere's second oldest democracy, has perhaps the most to gain from this. Latin American governments have a long history of being ruled by military commanders, often corrupt. Through interaction with the armed forces, SF soldiers reinforce the values of democracy and human rights. This may also act as a long-term benefit to Latin American governments by helping to eliminate one of the leading factors contributing to insurgent causes: government corruption. Likewise, this effect can have it a substantial impact for Afghanistan. By helping increase the professionalism of the Afghan National Army, SOF may help the country end warlordism through the disbandment of the tribal militias.

The Warlord Problem

Ending the reign of the warlords in Afghanistan has the benefit of denying sanctuary to narcotraffickers and contributing to the elimination of government corruption. Warlords are merely commanders of tribal militia, and most are fulfilling a role akin to local government. In Millen's Strategy Research Project, he states some of the reasons warlordism is so prevalent in Afghanistan. "A product of numerous historical invasions and compartmentalized geography, Afghan society is actually a quilt-work of 'village states' comprising various tribes and ethnicities" (Millen 2005, 5). More than thirty years of war in Afghanistan have left the fledgling central government unable to provide all the necessary services most citizens expect, such as security in the form of local police. In many cases it is the warlords who provide the local law enforcement.

37

While most warlords may have their ethnic tribes' best interests at heart, little to no government oversight often leads to corruption.

Warlords gained their initial strength from superpower patronage during the Soviet-Afghan war. Warlords such as Abdul Rashid Dostam, leader of the ethnic Uzbeks in northern Afghanistan, originally gained influence as a supporter of the Soviets, who supplied him with tanks. Ten years later, Dostam was an integral member of the Northern Alliance, led by Ahmed Shah Massoud, who was also known as the Lion of the Panjshir for his brave actions against the Soviets. Massoud was assassinated by Taliban operatives on 9 September 2001, an effort to deal a final blow to the Northern Alliance, and it would be Dostam who provided the largest indigenous forces when the US invaded Afghanistan. To his credit, Dostam recognized the opportunity to turn over his warlord powers to the new central government and become involved in the nascent democracy. While Dostam provides an example of a warlord co-opted into the new government, Gulbuddin Hekmatyar provides the counterpoint.

Hekmatyar was in the CIA's favor during the Afghan-Soviet war because he proved extremely successful in battle, and the CIA was willing to look the other way when Hekmatyar would smuggle opium out of Afghanistan on his runs to pick up US-supplied weapons to fight the Soviets. However, Hekmatyar did not begin using the opium trade to the extent he does today until the CIA funding dried up after the Soviet retreat in 1989 (Chouvy 2004, 2). Millen makes the argument that without government oversight many warlords follow Hekmatyar's example and use the opium trade to finance their militias. "Warlords and militia leaders are able to shroud their troop strengths by paying their militiamen with profits from the illicit opium trade" (Millen 2005, 4).

However, given the relative broad nature of Millen's Strategy Research Project, he does not elaborate or give specific examples of other warlords who may use narcotrafficking to their financial benefit. Likewise, the CRS report also comes to the same conclusion, "The continuing survival of warlords and regional militia, some of whom benefit directly from the narcotics trade, remains a significant challenge to the authority of Afghanistan's elected government as well as to the general security and stability of the country and its population" (2004, 6). Regardless of how many warlords are connected with narcotrafficking, warlordism remains one more barrier that all interested partners will have to face before the opium trade is eradicated in Afghanistan.

So far it seems as if Karzai's understanding of the tribal alliances in Afghanistan is paying off. The more militia leaders he can invite into the government peacefully the less likely those leaders will remain or become involved in narcotrafficking. As noted above, Karzai recognizes the implications of Afghanistan becoming a narco state and he is attempting to use all strategies at his disposal to rid himself and the country of the problem.

Likewise, the military recognizes the magnitude of the problem and the need to stop the flow of narcotics from Afghanistan. Supreme Allied Commander, Europe and Commander of the United States European Command General James Jones stated,

> the number one problem. . .is narcotics. . . .it's not the resurgence of the Taliban or al-Qaida. But we will devise a system for counter operations, the offensive operations, that there will be adequate forces to do that from nations who are willing to do that. . . . It will not just be done in the east, it will not just be done in the south, but it will be a national effort that forces that are highly mobile and capable of doing that kind of operation can be inserted where they're required to conduct those kinds of operations (2005, 6).

The problem lies in the assumption by news media, such as in the *Time* article

mentioned above, that the military should play a larger role. As noted earlier, real success

can only be accomplished through a thoroughly holistic approach, that is, all instruments

of national power, and host-nation and coalition partner integration. From a US

perspective this means a comprehensive IA strategy.

<u>Interagency Coordination in Afghanistan</u>

IA activities in Afghanistan are indeed comprehensive as the DOS's "Plan

Afghanistan" initiative mentioned in the CRS report above alludes to. Within the DOS

the burden of CN activities falls upon State's Bureau for International Narcotics and Law

Enforcement Affairs (INL), which is increasingly assisting Afghan CN efforts. The INL

website homepage includes in its mission statement, "Counternarcotics and anticrime

programs also complement the war on terrorism, both directly and indirectly, by

promoting modernization of and supporting operations by foreign criminal justice

systems and law enforcement agencies charged with the counter-terrorism mission"

(DOS 2006). According to Nancy J. Powell, Acting Assistant Secretary for International

Narcotics and Law Enforcement Affairs, the "INL plays a key role in carrying out the

President's National Drug Control Strategy by leading the development and

implementation of U.S. international drug control efforts" (2005, 1).

The current US Afghan CN policy was summarized by Powell in testimony to the

House Armed Services Committee on 22 June 2005.

> Together with the United Kingdom (UK), which has the lead on
> coordinating international counternarcotics (CN) assistance in Afghanistan, and
> with other donors, we are increasing our support for the Government of
> Afghanistan's anti-drug efforts. Experience elsewhere shows that only a holistic
> approach, one that combines negative consequences for participating in the drug

40

trade with legal alternative income options and a vigorous public education campaign, can succeed in shrinking the drug trade and turning the public against it. In coordination with the UK, Germany (which has the lead on international police assistance to Afghanistan) and Italy (which has the lead on international assistance for justice reform), the United States is implementing a comprehensive five-pillar counternarcotics (CN) program that covers law enforcement, interdiction, eradication, alternative livelihood projects and public information campaigns. (2005, 2)

This statement highlights some essential elements of the US government's CN efforts. First, international cooperation and coordination are vital to ensuring the legitimacy of the Afghan government. Powell mentions in additional congressional testimony, "In accordance with the Bonn agreement, responsibility for different realms of Afghan stabilization was divided between the United States and our allies" (2005, 2) She continues, "The United Kingdom is the lead-nation for counternarcotics, the Federal Republic of Germany is the lead-nation for police programs, and Italy is the lead-nation for justice programs" (2005, 2). According to the author's research, however, the actual Bonn Agreement document yielded no such delineation. However, Assistant Secretary of Defense for Special Operations and Low Intensity Conflict Thomas O'Connell as well suggested the allies agreed on such matters at the Bonn Agreement on 5 December 2001, but he also could not find any mention within the actual document. Regardless, it is a matter of fact these countries are responsible for the aforementioned "different realms." Without full commitment from these North Atlantic Treaty Organization (NATO) members the Afghan population may not support the five-pillar program. At the very least, citizens might believe anticoalition propaganda that the Afghan government is only a puppet of US intentions if only US governmental agencies were combating the opium trade. That is not to say the US is not assisting Kabul with OGA support with subject matter experts in the various fields discussed. For example, Italy, the lead county for

41

justice reform, receives assistance from US DOJ personnel, as well as providing its own experts to help build capacity in the Afghan justice system.

Second, the testimony emphasizes the need for a holistic approach. It is encouraging that senior US officials are aware of this need to address the totality of the problem. Powell comments, "robust drug production contributes to an environment of corruption and of political and economic instability, and thereby threatens the democratically elected Afghan Government" (2005, 1). Third, the excerpt concisely delineates the lead government missions and the division of assistance to the Government of Afghanistan. Again, although a nation may be designated the lead in international assistance, this does not imply it is rendering its assistance unilaterally. For the US part, it is truly an IA effort. In the example above of Italy, the DOJ may provide the personnel to assist Italian subject matter experts, but DOJ is being funded with DOS coffers through the INL CN program. This is important in that it is nearly unprecedented within the American bureaucracy. Fiscal jurisdictions are legislatively defined, and seldom has a program of this magnitude been able to cut through the Beltway red tape to the benefit of IA cooperation.

Finally, this testimony discusses the five-pillar CN program. Analysis of each pillar will provide a better grasp of this holistic approach and how coordination and cooperation are handled among Afghanistan, coalition partners, and US IA activities. Each pillar will be discussed at length. Figure 1 graphically depicts the five pillars, built on the foundation of the coalition partners supporting the Afghan CN initiative, and further supported by the major US agencies. The pillars are supporting the Afghan agencies, and they, in turn, support the Afghan government. The US and Afghan agencies depicted are roughly grouped to correspond to the pillars they support.

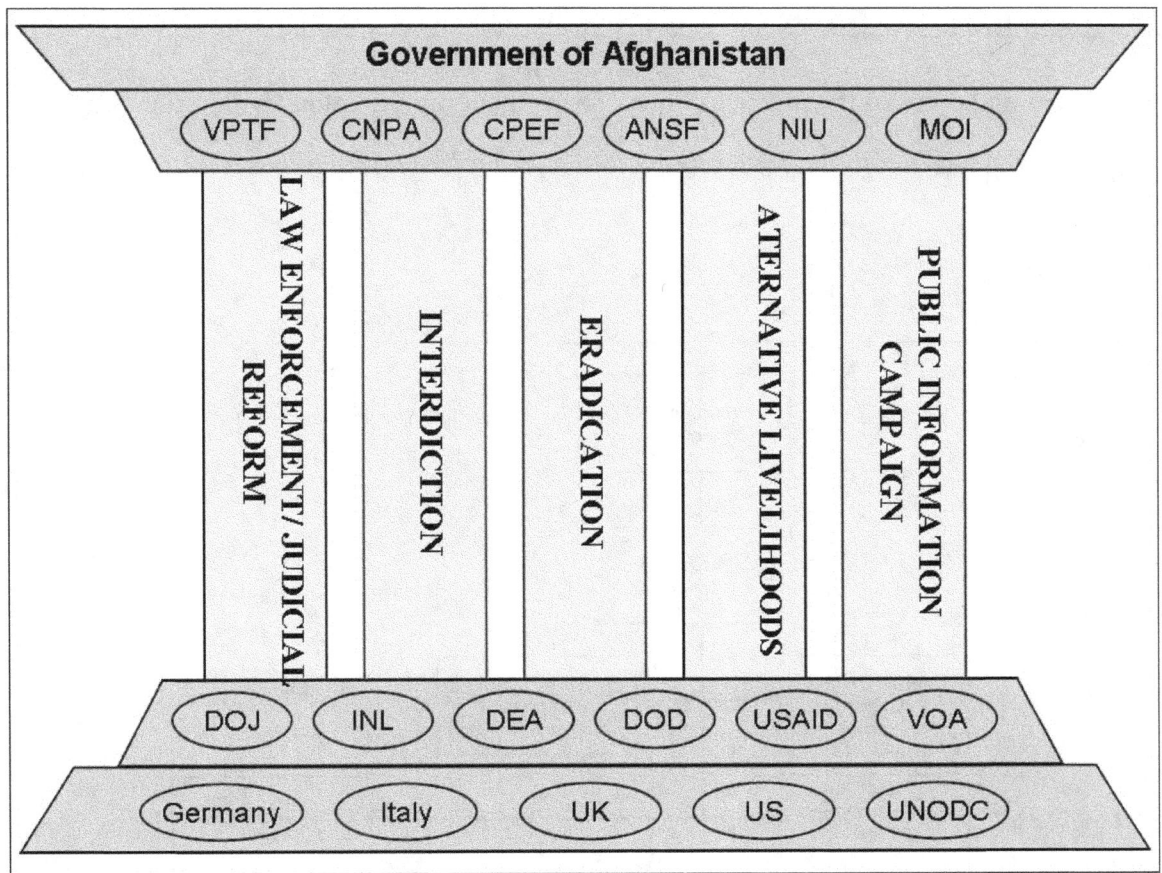

Figure 1.   Afghanistan Five-Pillar Counternarcotics Plan

Law Enforcement

The "INL assists lead-nation Germany in helping the GOA [Government of Afghanistan] develop a competent, professional, democratic, police force with the necessary training, equipment, infrastructure, institutional capacity and organizational structure to enforce the rule of law" (Powell 2005, 2). Specifically, the INL is training 50,000 national police and 12,000 border police. As of September 2005, more than

43

45,000 police officers have been trained, as well as approximately 3,000 border guards and 1,100 highway patrol police. These police are being trained at the Central Training Center in Kabul supported by Regional Training Centers in Gardez, Mazar-e Sharif, Kandahar, Konduz, Jalalabad and Heart (Powell 2005, 4). See figure 2 for the organizational chart of the major CN law enforcement organizations within the Afghan Ministry of Interior.

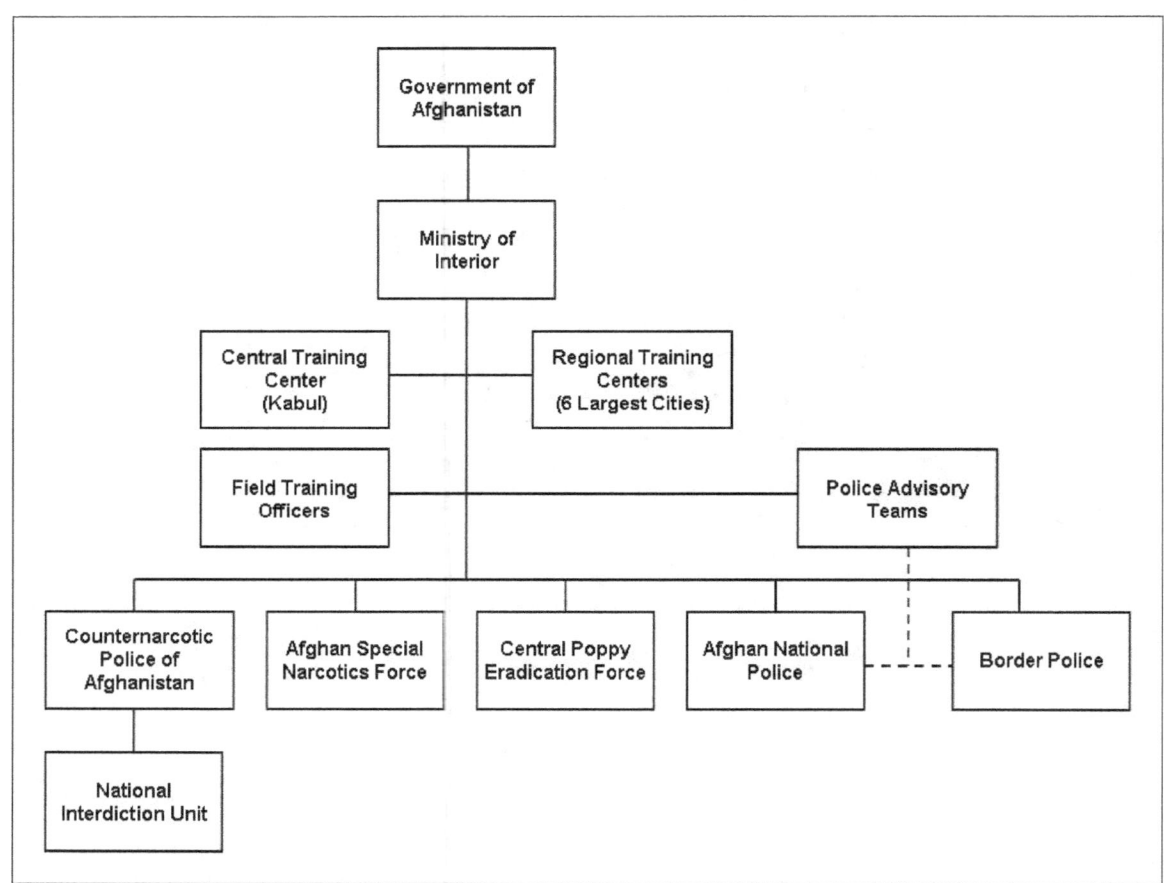

Figure 2.   Significant Afghan Counternarcotics Law Enforcement Forces

The DOS developed a field training officers program as the next step in supporting reform in the Afghan Ministry of Interior. This program was established to assist Afghan police trainees in transitioning from the institutional learning objectives to field work. Initiated in Kabul, the goal is "to expand the effort nationwide to ensure that police receive the monitoring, evaluation and feedback necessary to complete their training" (Powell 2005, 2). Deployable police advisory teams will provide the advanced training and mentoring to the Afghan field training officers once they have completed their field training. This fact is important to note because it demonstrates the desire for continuous training and development within the Afghan law enforcement institution.

Beyond the entry-level training provided at the Regional Training Centers, the practical application training of the field training officers and the continuous mentoring of the police advisory teams, the INL has also identified the need for reform initiatives to maintain the Afghan momentum to "transition into a professional, democratic police organization" (Powell 2005, 3). These initiatives "address organizational reform and help develop revenue-generating initiatives, establish community policing projects and other important projects such as anti-corruption initiatives" (Powell 2005, 3). Part of this organizational reform is designed to bring the Afghan police on par with the Afghan National Army through pay and rank restructuring, and to eliminate the bureaucratic nepotism indicative of the original organization.

These entry-level initiatives form the backbone of a professional police corps, a necessary step to creating the Counternarcotics Police of Afghanistan. The UNODC, the UK, and INL have assisted in the Counternarcotics Police of Afghanistan's development and its three sections: investigation, intelligence, and interdiction.

Noting the perniciousness of Afghanistan's opium trade, one of the first institutions to be given fast track priorities within the criminal justice and corrections

45

sectors was the Counternarcotics Vertical Prosecution Task Force (VPTF). The INL remains the lead US agency accountable for the program; however, the DOJ is supporting the program by assigning federal prosecutors to the VPTF to assist Afghan judges and prosecutors in bringing to court narcotics cases. In this capacity, DOJ has assisted the VPTF in the "drafting of money laundering, asset forfeiture, extradition and narcotics laws" (Powell 2005, 3). This aspect of justice reform plays a significant role in the law enforcement pillar. In addition to the criminal justice reform there is also a corrections infrastructure improvement aspect.

Supporting the VPTF will be the Counternarcotics Justice Center. DOD is building the justice center in Kabul to serve as a secure court and detention center, out of which the task force will operate. The detention center will hold those individuals who have been indicted on CN charges and are awaiting trial. The Counternarcotics Justice Center will also serve as the incarceration facility for convicted CN criminals until a new CN prison is built.

Criminal law education is also a key component to the Afghan legal reform measures, and as such the US is instituting the US-Afghanistan Masters of Law Program. This fully-funded program allows Afghan law professors to attend a US law school in order to help professionalize the legal system. Additional legal reform is being led by the Italian government, where efforts are being focused on the National Legal Training Center. The training center is being built by the United Nations Office for Project Services with funding by the Italian government. Its charter is to "strengthen the capacity of judicial actors in delivering justice throughout the country" (UN 2004, 3) by providing "a centralized resource for specialized training, licensing, and accreditation of Afghan lawyers and judges" (Powell 2005, 5).

Finally, two additional programs are being assisted by IA partners. The Justice Sector Support Program and the Corrections System Support Program. The Justice Sector Support Program is a national-level institutional capacity-building venture designed to assist the Afghan Ministry of Justice and Attorney General's Office. Under the program, the training of the Afghan legal tripartite-- judges, prosecutors, and defense attorneys--is to be standardized. The Corrections System Support Program assists the national corrections system in a similar manner, but primarily in the realm of infrastructure development.

Interdiction

There are two primary Afghan organizations specifically chartered to implement the interdiction pillar: the Afghan Special Narcotics Force and the Afghan National Interdiction Unit (NIU). The Afghan Special Narcotics Force has been active since 2004, and in that year it destroyed seventy heroin labs, eighty-one metric tons of opium, and twenty-eight metric tons of precursor chemicals. The NIU is to be incorporated into the Counternarcotics Police of Afghanistan eventually (see Figure 2); however, it currently remains a unilateral organization. Initial NIU training was conducted by DOD personnel, although continuing mentorship has been handed off to DEA foreign-deployed advisory and support teams. Through this program, approximately one-hundred NIU officers have completed a six-week training course and are conducting operations in the field with DEA advisors. Six female officers also graduated from this course. This is significant because the Afghan culture forbids male officers from searching female suspects. The

47

creation of the NIU is a capacity-building initiative and, with DEA assistance, "will help

with the destruction of existing opium storage sites, clandestine heroin processing labs,

and precursor chemical supplies" (Braun 2005, 3). It is important to note that this IA

approach has resulted in coordination and synchronization among Afghan NIU forces,

DEA advisors, and the US military. One example of this integration was an operation

conducted on 15 March 2005 in the Nangarhar province in which this combined, joint,

and IA task force raided three drug labs, destroying two metric tons of opium in this one

operation alone.

One of the most successful aspects of the interdiction pillar has been Operation

Containment, which has been running continuously since 2002. In order to process opium

into heroin precursor chemicals are needed. None of these compounds are produced

within Afghanistan itself. Thus, if the importation of these chemicals from neighboring

countries could be disrupted, heroin production could be affected. Operation Containment

is an "intensive, multi-national program . . . initiated in an attempt to place a security belt

around Afghanistan, which would prevent processing chemicals from entering the

country and opium and heroin from leaving" (Braun 2005, 4). It is a massive effort

involving nineteen countries in Central Asia, the Caucuses, the Middle East, Europe and

Russia (Braun 2005, 4).

The quantitative results from the operation are impressive. In 2002 only 407

kilograms of heroin were seized coming out of Afghanistan. In FY 2004, this figure

jumped to 14.9 metric tons, a 3661 percent increase. Additionally, other seizures that year

were recorded; 7700 kilograms of morphine base, 5900 kilograms of opium gum, 3270

kilograms of precursor chemicals. Also eleven heroin labs were destroyed, and 498 individuals were arrested. The latest figures available during this research were for the first quarter of FY 2005, which showed still additional increases in the amount of drugs seized. Three thousand kilograms of opium gum were confiscated, an increase in 203 percent when adjusted on an annual basis (Braun 2005, 4).

The Chief of Operations for the DEA, Michael A. Braun, testified before the House Committee on International Relations on 17 March 2005 and summarized the effects of Operation Containment on terrorist groups.

> In the past, terrorist groups derived much of their funding and support from state sponsors; however, with increased international pressure, many of these sources have become less reliable and, in some instances, disappeared altogether. As a result, terrorist groups have turned to alternative sources of financing, including fundraising from sympathizers and non-governmental organizations, as well as criminal activities, such as arms trafficking, money laundering, kidnap-for-ransom, extortion, racketeering, and drug trafficking. Both criminal organizations and terrorist groups continue developing international networks and establishing alliances of convenience. In the new era of globalization, both terror and crime organizations have expanded and diversified their activities, taking advantage of the internationalization of communications and banking systems, as well as the opening of borders. As a result, the traditional boundaries between terrorists groups and other criminal groups have begun to blur. (2005, 23)

If Braun's assertions are correct, perhaps the current five-pillar model of IA CN cooperation is sufficient to have an impact on Afghanistan's opium dependency and disrupt one of al Qaeda's main sources of funding. Certainly there is more work to be done; however, Braun seems optimistic regarding the outcome.

Eradication

Essential to the opium eradication effort is the Afghan CPEF. The CPEF is a predominately INL-funded institution under the Poppy Elimination Program. Eventually the CPEF will become reorganized into the Afghan Eradication Force. Currently, CPEF

49

teams are comprised of approximately eight to ten police and international advisors. There are approximately 500 Afghan police officers currently working on the many CPEF teams. While directed from the central government, they "deploy to the seven major producing provinces (Kandahar, Nangarhar, Uruzgan, Farah, Badakhshan, Helmand, and Balkh) to mobilize and assist provincial officials in conducting an effective public information campaign, to discourage poppy planting, and to implement provincial eradication programs early enough for farmers to replant fields with legitimate crops" (Powell 2005, 3).

Unfortunately, the forced eradication efforts have been met with hostility during the first two years the program has been in effect and the results were less than hoped for. The UNODC estimates only 5,100 hectares or 5 percent of the annual opium yield was eradicated despite most of 2005's efforts being focused in the two largest opium producing provinces, Nangarhar and Helmand (2005, 9). Working in conjunction with the Government of Afghanistan and the CPEF, DOS has identified lessons learned from the failures of 2005 and is working to implement the changes to make the Poppy Eradication Program a viable pillar in Afghanistan's CN plan. One of the changes is greater coordination and assistance from DOD, the NIU and the CPEF. Specifically, DOD has begun training NIU and CPEF helicopter pilots to enhance their ability to identify and monitor opium crops.

Alternative Livelihoods

The IA Afghanistan AL program is led by USAID, with assistance from DOS, and largely funded by international organizations and foreign governments. It is a "comprehensive, multi-year USAID-supported development program . . . [to] promote the cultivation of high-value licit crops, develop rural credit markets as well as financial and business development services, rehabilitate rural infrastructure, develop new internal and export markets for Afghan products, and remove administrative barriers that constrain businesses" (Powell 2005, 4). As this testimony implies, the AL program encompasses more than assisting farmers in developing alternative crops.

USAID is promoting cash-for-work programs, which give farmers immediate sources of income, an incentive-based approach which combats the problem of farmers having to wait until harvest season to earn income. Cash-for-work programs include irrigation, canal network improvements, and infrastructure projects. Additionally, during these projects workers are made aware of seed and fertilizer distribution centers, where farmers can go and receive these items. At the same time farmers are picking up seed, antipoppy messages are disseminated, ensuring a wide distribution of the CN theme. Other USAID initiatives are crop diversification and fruit and nut processing.

USAID's efforts are integrated into the development framework directly through field officers working with the provisional reconstruction teams. While USAID is formally responsible for the overall stability and reconstruction of Afghanistan through economic development, its initiatives are important aspects of Afghanistan's CN strategy.

Public Information

The goal of the CN public information campaign is to educate a largely uninformed Afghan public on the illegality of opium cultivation and hazards opium presents to public health. Powell notes the prominent role that President Karzai has played in continuingly addressing the negative impact of opium on the country. DOS is again leading the IA public information efforts through the use of foreign assistance

51

funding. However, both the British Broadcasting Corporation and the Voice of America play important roles in reaching a largely illiterate populace in the rural areas by broadcasting antidrug messages in various dialects. These messages and other DOS public information efforts are coordinated through Afghanistan's Ministry of Interior and Ministry of Counternarcotics with the aim of reducing opium cultivation, trade, and use.

More specifically, in 2005, "nearly 4,000 broadcasts of counternarcotics messages (were) aired on more than thirty radio stations, with an estimated audience of about 20 million people in the primary poppy-growing provinces and beyond. This program has also led to the distribution of 2000 posters, 170,000 stickers, and 200,000 matchbook covers with counternarcotics messages in these same provinces" (Powell 2005, 2). One method of determining the effectiveness of this program can be through the review of the UNODC's Farmers' Intention Survey, which was analyzed at the beginning of this chapter. Thirty-one percent of farmers who grew poppies in 2004 and did not in 2005 said they were dissuaded from doing so by the Afghan government's poppy ban.

Beyond the Five Pillars

Successful CN strategies are time-intensive operations, coordinated through multiple governments and agencies in a holistic manner that addresses multiple lines of operations, such as the DOS-led Five Pillars Program. Within such a strategy the military instrument of national power has one of the smallest roles, yet perhaps the broadest range of capabilities with which to assist the implementation of the diplomatic, informational and economic instruments of national power. Given this fact, one of the greatest contributions to the CN strategy the military can provide the IA efforts that have not been discussed yet is the creation of intelligence fusion centers.

According to the CRS study, *Afghanistan: Narcotics and U.S. Policy*, "Defense Department and military personnel plan to focus future efforts on further improving Afghanistan's border security and providing greater intelligence support to Afghan law enforcement officials through joint military/DEA/Afghan 'intelligence fusion centers' located at U.S. facilities in Kabul and the Afghan Ministry of Interior" (2005, 33). Without the capacity to exchange information, each agency is reliant only on information gathered by sources under their control. A fusion center allows the agencies to maximize their efforts and surge resources and capabilities to engage the common threat with the most appropriate means.

It is perhaps in this sense that the secondary and tertiary questions of this thesis are best answered. Subject matter experts of Afghanistan's CN strategy have identified two of the weaknesses of the IA approach as being the lack of intelligence sharing and failure to coordinate their actions. The intelligence fusion cell is one example of the effort to make institutional changes that will improve the capabilities of those involved. It is important that so many agencies are involved in the CN fight; however, these agencies lack the institutional ability to fully integrate their efforts. The intelligence fusion cells are an example of a more efficient and effective method of employing IA capabilities in the CN strategy.

SOF, and in particular SF, provide two important capabilities when incorporated into the intelligence fusion cell. The first is their ability to train Afghanistan's military and paramilitary operators in CN operations under the foreign internal defense training program. SF teams training Afghan forces can act as a conduit for the intelligence fusion cells, guiding Afghans where the intelligence dictates CN forces should act. The second is the intelligence-gathering capabilities inherent in SF operations. SF soldiers are less likely than their conventional counterparts to be confined to forward operating bases from which they conduct their operations. They interact with Afghanis, the tribal elders, and co-opted militia leaders to gain their trust and support for their ongoing operations against Taliban insurgents and al Qaeda fighters. Through this interaction SF teams can also find ways to elicit information regarding local opium crops, forwarding this information to the intelligence fusion cells or acting on this information themselves with their Afghan counterparts. It might even be enough for SF team to assist the AL program and public information campaign by dissuading local leaders or farmers from supporting opium cultivation within their area of operation. As US forces rotate out Afghanistan as part of the NATO agreement, a greater CN emphasis may be the purview of the NATO coalition partners, and in particular the UK.

The UK volunteered to be the lead government in the CN fight at the G-8 summit in 2003 (O'Connell 2005). Since then, the UK has coordinated the CN activities of all countries, and as the lead government, heads the four-nation Counter-Narcotics Working Group: Afghanistan, Pakistan, the US, and the UK. As the lead, the British military has contributed a more offensive posture in its conduct of CN operations. In particular, British SOF are assisting the Afghan Special Narcotics Force in conducting CN operations. However, the British government is not openly admitting Special Air Service (SAS) involvement. The British news organization The Guardian reported, "British officials are coy about discussing the SAS role in the ASNF [Afghan Special Narcotics Force] but claim it has succeeded in denting the countrywide drugs trade" (Wilson 2005, 1).

While the UK military may be taking a more offensive approach, the British government understands the lessons from the Latin American model and is following the holistic method. Additionally, officials recognize the fruition of their efforts will take years to visualize. British Ambassador to Kabul, Dr. Rosalind Mardsen, "reckoned completely cleansing the country of the drug menace would take a decade, a long-term process that could not be wrapped up in an ambitious sweep. The timeline given by the ambassador conforms to the UN Office on Drugs and Crime's plan" (Pahjwok Afghan News 2005).

CHAPTER 4

CONCLUSIONS AND RECOMMENDATIONS

Conclusions

The secondary question this thesis posed is how SOF can be used in support of CN operations without detracting from their current fight. As discussed in chapter 3, SF have a long history of conducting CN operations. Although a majority of this effort has been concentrated in Latin America, where SF soldiers do not have the primary responsibility to destroy antigovernment forces, it is their ancillary goal of training the host-nation military to do just that. This is how SF can significantly contribute to a CN strategy through these activities when combined with a comprehensive government-led, IA-backed CN strategy, as evidenced by the global reduction in coca supply.

Since the beginning of the GWOT, SOF have been conducting combat operations at a higher operational tempo than ever before. Due to the demands of multiple deployments to numerous countries few commanders want to task their teams with additional missions. Therefore it is important to address how SF can support CN operations without detracting from their current activities. This may mean the implementation of a better conduit for the reporting of passive intelligence, such as civil affairs soldiers observing narcotraffickers while helping to install a new water pump in a rural village, or hearing of a heroin lab while overseeing the construction of a new school. The intelligence fusion cell, once fully implemented, should be the exact medium to filter such reports from the field.

As mentioned previously, SF teams are perhaps best suited to support the intelligence fusion cells with actionable intelligence. During the course of their daily

56

operations SF soldiers routinely engage Afghanis to develop contacts and information needed to conduct their operations. When this information is passed back to their higher headquarters, any information concerning the opium trade could easily be passed along to the intelligence fusion cell to be vetted. If immediate action is required, the SF team that gathered the information may be in the best position to conduct an operation to disrupt the activity. If there is any concern that this may damage the team's relationship with the source of the information, then the information should be passed to the CPEF, which due to the coalition nature of the intelligence fusion cell, would have access to the information. Finally, SF can further assist the Afghan CN operations through their continued training of the Afghan CN forces.

The answer to the tertiary question was partially identified in the analysis of previous question. The robust nature of the IA CN strategy appears to be the right approach to eventually eliminating Afghanistan's dependency on opium and disrupting al Qaeda's illicit funding. It also appears that those agencies that are integral in the CN strategy recognize what improvements need to be made and implement changes for the better. One of these changes has been the creation of the joint IA, and multinational intelligence fusion cell. This change will work to eliminate the "stove-piping" or hierarchical manner in which information is evaluated and shared to ensure the proper individuals or agencies collaborate on CN operations.

The primary question this thesis posed is whether the current model of IA CN cooperation is sufficient to have an impact on Afghanistan's opium dependency and disrupt one of al Qaeda's main sources of funding. The facts discussed herein identified that current model of Afghanistan's CN strategy and showed the vast network of cooperation among Afghanistan, foreign governments, international organizations, and US IA and military institutions. While fair criticism might be why these organizations were not addressed immediately after Karzai's government was established, it should be appreciated that they were soon afterward, but met with severe setbacks in the beginning due to the pervasive nature of opium cultivation within Afghanistan.

There is no easy solution to overcome the Afghan opium trade quickly, and many experts recognize the CN strategy must be a holistic one and one with a long-term approach. If Afghanistan were to conduct a massive CN undertaking in one province one season, farmers and traffickers there would only rely on other provinces until the CPEF moved on, and then would start right back up again. In this sense it is imperative that the Afghan law enforcement institutions be rebuilt with the capacity to engage this threat year after year in every region. Likewise, farmers need incentives to plant alternative crops and, through a public information campaign, they need to understand the repercussions of cultivating opium.

Since the emphasis is on a long-term solution, the immediate effects of the CN strategy may not be readily seen in the next few years, yet already one can see a slight trend away from the opium industry in Afghanistan, as noted in the UNODC documents. Only through continued pressure from all the IA actors will Afghanistan have the capacity to ensure the hazards of the opium trade will be defeated forever. Given this understanding it appears that the current model of IA CN cooperation is robust enough to make an impact on Afghanistan's opium dependency.

Recommendations

IA CN activities have evolved from individual agencies conducting unilateral missions into a comprehensive coordinated Afghan strategy. Through a combination of Afghani, coalition, IA and military cells, and working groups and task forces, a synchronized, successful strategy has emerged to combat narcotrafficking over time. However, some problems do remain.

One of the principal reasons for the ineffectiveness of the earlier CN strategy was the lack of IA funding and staffing required for such a massive undertaking. For the most part, funding for DOD and DOS are legislatively bound by US legal codes Title 10 and 22, respectively. Seldom are funds allocated to one agency allowed to be used for operations of the other. Defense garners the largest percentage of the US budget, with $419.3 billion for FY 2006; State is allocated $31.8 billion. Given the scope of responsibility that DOS has for Afghanistan's reconstruction, this seems to be a significant disparity. One method for increasing the DOS share is through several alternative funding methods, where DOD is able to fund projects in which DOS has the lead. Two of these funding initiatives are the Commander's Emergency Response Program and the Overseas Humanitarian Disaster Relief Assistance and Civic Aid funds. In a time when DOD and OGAs are increasingly conducting coordinated missions in a joint IA environment, further methods need to be streamlined to surge fiscal capacity beyond the Commander's Emergency Response Program and Overseas Humanitarian Disaster Relief Assistance and Civic Aid workarounds in order to effectively leverage all the instruments of national power.

In addition to being underfunded for the plethora of missions, and perhaps because of this, many OGAs are understaffed. Personnel are unavailable to fill all of the duty positions that are required to meet the global objectives of the agencies. Additionally, unlike the military, agencies cannot compel their personnel to deploy to hazardous duty locations, relying instead on volunteers within the organization. These personnel serve relatively short tours when compared to the military, tasking additional staff to backfill the positions, and creating a greater strain on an already stressed staff.

Also, these agencies have little or no organic capability to deploy personnel to austere locations. Thus, they rely on either the military or resources outside of their respective agencies to deploy. This presents military commanders with the dilemma to either assist governmental agencies or push forward their own personnel, logistics, or needed equipment. In the case of civilian transport, agencies are constrained to the existing air infrastructure, something lacking early on in Afghanistan or Iraq.

A common refrain in the discussion about a more efficient and effective method of employing IA activities is that legislation is required that mandates agencies to cooperate and synchronize their operations. Similar legislation was passed in 1986 requiring the military's various services to do just this in a joint environment. This legislation is known as the Goldwater-Nichols Defense Reorganization Act. Among other things, this legislation enabled the interoperability of the service components so that they could effectively and efficiently shoot, move, and communicate together in the same area of operation. However, perhaps the most significant outcome of this legislation is the designation of supporting and supported relationships within the services. By establishing which component has the lead in a particular operation, unity of command and unity of effort are achieved. An IA Goldwater-Nichols Act would do likewise, and in this case by empowering the designated lead agency in the CN fight, it would establish a synchronizing capability to maximize efforts across the IA spectrum.

In the interim, cells, working groups, and task forces work around this issue and are imperative to coordinating the IA CN process. However, in the long term it is necessary to address this issue to better integrate and empower the IA actors. As it stands, most agencies are united in their strategic goals, that is, eliminating Afghan's opium dependency, but occasionally the tactical goals are at odds with one another.

Another important outcome of the Goldwater-Nichols Act is the broader development of joint doctrine. This provides the services with a common terminology and framework for working in a joint environment. Currently, government agencies lack this common doctrine and therefore lack a common framework with which to synchronize and coordinate their activities.

A short note must also be made of IA rivalries. Just like the service rivalries that existed at the time the Goldwater-Nichols Act was established, government agencies have a natural tendency to seek credit for a particular operation or method in an effort to enhance their clout and perhaps receive a larger budget in future fiscal years.

It should be evident that the issues surrounding IA legislation should be studied further in order to create a more efficient and effective method of employing IA partners in the future. For the time being, the strength of these agencies lies in the personnel assigned to them, who have an honest belief in how their actions support the strategic goals. It is these people who developed the concepts of working groups, cells and task forces in order to effectively support the Afghan CN strategy.

Areas for Further Research

Finally, one area of the CN fight that has a direct impact on terrorist illicit funding is the financial aspect. As mentioned in the beginning of this thesis, the current US National Security Strategy states that one of the four areas of focus in the war on terrorism is the financial facet. The US Department of Treasury is contributing to the GWOT by doing just this. Treasury is a founding member of the multinational Financial Action Task Force. The Financial Action Task Force was originally created in 1989 by sixteen member nations to combat the global problem of money laundering. The charter was amended in 2001 to include action against terrorist financing as a means to disrupt global terrorist networks. This body based this inclusion on the UN Security Council Resolution 1373, which called for the prevention and suppression of the financing of terrorist acts.

The significance of targeting terrorist financing after 11 September 2001 was made public when President Bush announced that the first salvo in the GWOT was the seizure of terrorist funds by Treasury officials. In many ways, this is the hidden side of the war, that is, the continued pressure from Financial Action Task Force and other organizations has severely disrupted terrorist financing capabilities and the ability to trace certain accounts have led to several arrests of high ranking terrorist personnel. Thus, the direct targeting of terrorist financing is an important aspect in destroying organizations like al Qaeda, and, as such, would be a worthy topic for future research.

Lastly, Afghanistan's holistic CN strategy is on the correct track for success with coalition US military, interagency and financial support. There are aspects of the strategy which could be improved upon to make it a more efficient and effective. However, some of those changes are being implemented already. Afghan opium production was down in 2005 due to the measures currently in place, but the CN effort to eliminate Afghanistan's opium dependency will take years to become fully realized. Due to the nature in which al Qaeda and its associated networks depend on Afghanistan's opium industry, disrupting the narco trade is another means to disrupt terrorist operations and should be pursued as an integral part of the GWOT. Finally, the US is not alone in this venture, as President Karzai knows well. With the continued integration of Afghanistan's institutions and coalition support the CN fight will succeed.

REFERENCE LIST

Afghanistan Counter Narcotics Directorate. 2003. National Drug Control Strategy. Website. Original Afghanistan Transitional Authority website no longer available. Current National Drug Control Strategy available from http://www.mcn.gov.af/english/Documents.htm. Accessed on 12 October 2005.

Alliot-Marie, Michele. 2005. Committed to Kabul. *The Wall Street Journal*, 21 July, A10.

Blanchard, Christopher M. 2005. Afghanistan: Narcotics and U.S. Policy. *Congressional Research Service Report for Congress*. Fort Belvoir, VA: Defense Acquisition University, 26 May.

Blanchfield, Mike. 2002. Why Afghanistan's Poppy Fields Continue To Flourish. The Ottawa Citizen. 26 May. Newspaper on-line. Available from http://www.canada.com/ottawacitizen/index.html. Internet. Accessed on 12 October 2005.

Bogdanos, Matthew F. 2005. Joint Interagency Cooperation: The First Step. *Joint Force Quarterly* no. 37 (2nd Quarter): 10.

Bowden, Mark. 2001. *Killing Pablo*. New York, NY: Atlantic Monthly Press.

Braun, Michael A. 2005. Statement before the House International Relations Committee. 17 March. Database on-line. Available from http://wwwc.house.gov/international_relations/109/20058.pdf. Internet. Accessed on 20 February 2006.

Bush, George H. W. 1989. National Security Directive 18. 21 August. Databse on-line. Available from http://bushlibrary.tamu.edu/research/nsd/NSD/NSD%2018/0001.pdf. Internet. Accessed on 4 March 2006.

Charles, Robert. 2006. CENTCOM, Drugs and Afghanistan. *The Washington Times*, 25 January, 16.

Christian, Shirley. 1986. Bolivia Drug Traffic Builds Again as American Forces Withdraw. *The New York Times*, 2 December, A1.

Chouvy, Pierre-Arnaud. 2004. Narco-Terrorism in Afghanistan. *Terrorism Monitor* 2, no. 6 (25 March). Website. Available from http://www.geopium.org. Internet. Accessed on 18 September 2005.

Cole, Reyes. 2005. Drug Wars, Counterinsurgency and the National Guard. *Military Review* 85, no.6 (November-December): 70.

CRS. 2004. *See* Vaughn, Bruce, and Connie Veillete. 2004.

Department of the Army. 2001. Field Manual 3-05.20, *Special Forces Operations*. Washington, DC: US Government, 26 June.

Department of Defense. 1998. Joint Staff. JP 3-07.4, *Joint Counterdrug Operations*. Washington, DC: US Government, 17 February.

_____. 2001. Joint Staff. JP 1-02, *Department of Defense Dictionary of Military and Associated Terms*. Washington, DC: US Government.

FM 3-05.20. 2001. *See* Department of the Army. 2001.

Ghani, Ashraf. 2004. Where Democracy's Greatest Enemy Is a Flower. *The New York Times*, 11 December, A19.

Hertling, Mark P. 1990. Narcoterrorism: The New Unconventional War. *Military Review* 70, no. 3 (March): 16.

Hutchinson, Asa. 2002. Statement before the Senate Judiciary Committee. 13 March. Database on-line. Available from http://judiciary.senate.gov/testimony.cfm?id=196&wit_id=332. Internet. Accessed on 16 January 2006.

Joint Plan to Counter Drug Trafficking. 2005. *Dawn*. Website. Available from http://www.dawn.com/2005/10/06/nat20.htm. Internet. Accessed on 13 November 2005.

Jones, James. 2005. Statement at the European Command Headquarters. 20 October. Available from http://www.eucom.mil/english/Transcripts/20051020.asp. Internet. Accessed on 20 February 2006.

JP 1-02. 2001. *See* Department of Defense. 2001.

Kaplan, David E. 2005. Paying for Terror. *U.S. News & World Report*, 5 December, 40.

Labrousse, Alain. 2005. The FARC and the Taliban's Connection to Drugs. *Journal of Drug Issues* 35, no. 1 (winter): 169.

Lister, Richard. 2000. US Commits to Colombia. *BBC News*. Website. Available from http://news.bbc.co.uk/1/hi/world/americas/902035.stm. Internet. Accessed on 27 November 2005.

Mabry, Donald J. 1990. Andean Drug Trafficking and the Military Option. *Military Review* 70, no. 3 (March): 29.

McGirk, Tim. 2004. Terrorism's Harvest. *TIME Asia Magazine*. 2 August. Journal on-line. Available from http://www.time.com/time/asia/magazine/printout/0,13675,501040809-674806,00.html. Internet. Accessed 27 November 2005.

McGowen, Richard S. 2003. *Central Asian Drug Trafficking Dilemma*. Monterey, CA: US Naval Postgraduate School, December.

Millan, G. Joseph. 2005. *Afghanistan: Reconstituting a Collapsed State*. Carlisle Barracks, PA: Strategic Studies Institute, US Army War College, April.

_____. 2003. *Poppy Cultivation in Afghanistan: A Global, Strategic Nemesis*. Carlisle Barracks, PA: US Army War College, 7 April.

National Drug Control Strategy. 2003. *See* Afghanistan Counter Narcotics Directorate. 2003.

O'Connell, Thomas W. 2004. Statement before the Senate Committee on Armed Services. 25 March. Database on-line. Available from http://armed-services.senate.gov/statemnt/2004/ March/OConnell.pdf. Internet. Accessed on 6 January 2006.

Office of the President. 2002. *The National Security Strategy of the United States of America*. Washington, DC: US Government, September.

Olcott, Martha B., and Natalia Udalova. 2000. Drug Trafficking on the Great Silk Road. *Carnegie Endowment Working Papers* no. 11. Washington, DC, March.

Pajhwok Afghan News. 2005. UK Sees Drop in Poppy Cultivation in Afghanistan. 28 July. Journal on-line. Available from http://www.pajhwak.com/viewstory.asp? lng=eng&id=5747. Internet. Accessed on 27 November 2005.

Perito, Robert M. 2004. Testimony before the Senate Foreign Relations Committee. 12 May. Database on-line. Available from http://foreign.senate.gov/testimony/ 2004/PeritoTestimony040512.pdf. Internet. Accessed 27 November 2005.

Powell, Colin L. 1991. Statement before the Committee on Armed Services, US Senate. 21 February. Reprinted in *Fundamentals of Force Planning*. Vol. 2, *Defense Planning Cases*. 1991. Edited by the Force Planning Faculty Naval War College, Dr. Richmond M. Lloyd, et al. Newport, RI: Naval War College Press.

Powell, Nancy J. 2005. Testimony before the House Armed Services Committee. 22 June. Database on-line. Available from http://www.house.gov/hasc/schedules/ Powell-Afghan-Testimony.pdf. Internet. Accessed on 28 February 2006.

_____. 2005. Testimony before the House International Relations Committee. 22 September. Database on-line. Available from http://wwwc.house.gov/ international_relations/109/pow092205.pdf. Internet. Accessed on 28 February 2006.

Priest, Dana and Douglas Farah. 1998. U.S. Forces Training Troops in Colombia. *The Washington Post*, May 25, A01.

Quirk, Matthew. 2005. The New Opium War. *The Atlantic Monthly* 295, no. 2 (March): 52.

Reaves, Jackie L. 2003. *The Emerging Threat of Illicit Drug Funding of Terrorist Organizations*. Carlisle Barracks, PA: US Army War College, 7 April.

Scarborough, Rowan. 2004. Heroin Traffic Finances bin Laden. *The Washington Times*. 6 December. Newspaper on-line. Available from http://www.washington times.com/national/20041206-124320-5344r.htm. Internet. Accessed 27 November 2005.

Shanker, Thom. 2005. Pentagon Sees Antidrug Effort in Afghanistan. *The New York Times*, 25 May, A1.

Sharp, Walter. 2004. Testimony before the House Armed Services Committee. 29 April. Database on-line. Available from http://armedservices.house.gov/ openingstatementsandpressreleases/108thcongress/04-04-29sharp.html. Internet. Accessed on 20 February 2006.

Trumble, Roy R. 1991. *USSOCOM Support for Counter Narcotics*. Carlisle Barracks, PA: US Army War College, 21 March.

Tyson, Ann Scott. 2004. War on terror is also a war on drug traffic. *The Christian Science Monitor*, 18 February, 1.

United Nations Development Programme – Afghanistan. 2004. *Rebuilding the Justice Sector of Afghanistan*. Website on-line. Available from http://www.undp.org.af/ about_us/overview_undp_afg/dcse/prj_justice.htm. Internet. Accessed on 20 February 2006.

United Nations Office on Drugs and Crime. 2005. *Summary Findings of Opium Trends in Afghanistan, 2005*. New York, NY.

_____. 2005. *World Drug Report, 2005*. New York, NY.

US Agency for International Development. 2006. *Afghanistan Alternative Livelihoods Update* no. 10. March: 1.

US Army. Command and General Staff College. 2005. ST 20-10, *Master of Military Art and Science (MMAS) Research and Thesis*. Ft. Leavenworth, KS: USA CGSC, August.

US Department of Agriculture. Natural Resources Conservation Service. 2005. NRCS Sends Employees to Afghanistan. Website on-line. Available from http://www.nrcs.usda.gov/news/thisweek/2005/030905/afghanprts.html. Internet. Accessed on 23 March 2006.

US Department of State. 2006. Bureau for International Narcotics and Law Enforcement. Website on-line. Available from http://www.state.gov/p/inl/. Internet. Accessed on 16 January 2006.

US Drug Enforcement Agency. 2002. Drug Intelligence Brief. Database on-line. Available from http://www.dea.gov/pubs/intel/02039/02039.html. Internet. Accessed on 16 January 2006.

US Office of National Drug Control Policy. 2006. Available from http://www.whitehousedrug policy.gov/international/afghanistan.html. Internet. Accessed on 9 September 2005.

USA Today. 2005. Fighting kills 21 in Afghanistan. Journal on-line. Available from http://www.usa today.com. Internet. Accessed on 12 October 2005.

Vaughn, Bruce, and Connie Veillette. 2004. Foreign Affairs, Defense and Trade: Key Issues for the 109th Congress. *Congressional Research Service Report for Congress*. Fort Belvoir, VA: Defense Acquisition University, 27 December.

Watson, Paul. 2005. Afghanistan: A Harvest of Despair. *Los Angeles Times*, 29 May, A1.

Wilson, Jamie and Declan Walsh. 2005. Karzai accused of Being Soft on Opium Trade. *The Guardian*. 23 May. Journal on-line. Available from http://www.guardian. co.uk/afghanistan/story/0,,1489961,00.html. Internet. Accessed on 12 October 2005.

Zabriskie, Phil. 2006. Dangers up Ahead. *TIME Magazine*, 13 March, 36.